Printed in China

Maxim

箴言篇

林 立　陈爱明　李小艳　编译

韩清月　　　　　　　　　审校

外文出版社

卷首语

总有一种感动无处不在。

总有一种情怀轻舞飞扬。

总有一种生活, 在别处, 闪动异样的光芒。

阅读, 让我们的生活在情调与知性中享受更多……

故事与见闻, 犹如生活的魅力与智慧, 合着我们自身生命的光与影, 陪伴我们一路前行。

快乐和圆满, 幻想与失落, 飞扬的眼泪,行走江湖的落拓，不与人说的痛苦，渐行渐远的繁华，坚持的勇气，点点滴滴的小意思……

人生让我们感受到的，也许远远不只是这些；更多的是挫折后生长的力量，沉闷时的豁然开朗，是屋前那静静的南山上盛开的人淡如菊的境界，是闹市中跋涉红尘、豪情万丈的冲动，是很纯粹的一杯午后的香醇的咖啡……

漫步红尘，有彻悟来自他人的故事，有灵犀来自偶然的相遇，在这里，一种从未见过的却可能早就在我们心底的生活方式有可能与我们邂逅。

让我们一起阅读吧，感受生长的智慧、风雅与力量。

Contents

目 录

Wit

机智

A sense of humor is the ability to understand a joke and that the joke is oneself.

Clifton Paul Fadiman, American writer, editor
法迪曼，美国作家、编辑

A man that studieth revenge keeps his own wounds green.

Francis Bacon, English philosopher, statesman,
and essayist, 1561-1626
培根，英国哲学家、政治家、散文家

A classic is something that everybody wants to have read and nobody wants to read.

Mark Twain, American writer and humorist, 1835-1910
马克·吐温，美国作家、幽默家

A good marriage is at least 80 percent good luck in finding the right person at the right time. The rest is trust.

Nanette Newman, British Actress
纳内特·纽曼，英国女演员

A prudent question is one-half of wisdom.

Francis Bacon, English philosopher, statesman,
and essayist, 1561-1626
培根,英国哲学家、政治家、散文家

A man should be taller, older, heavier, uglier, and hoarser than his wife.

Edgar Watson Howe, American journalist, 1853-1937
豪,美国记者

A man who has never made a woman angry is a failure in life.

Christopher Morley, American actor, 1890-1957
克里斯托弗·莫利,美国作家

A sudden bold and unexpected question doth many times surprise a man and lay him open.

Francis Bacon, English philosopher, statesman,
and essayist, 1561-1626
培根,英国哲学家、政治家、散文家

A man's wife has more power over him than the state has.

Ralph Waldo Emerson, American author, 1803-1882
爱默生,美国作家

A **successful man** is one who makes more money than his wife can spend. A successful woman is one who can find such a man.

Lana Turner, American actress, 1921-1995

A good marriage would be between a blind wife and a deaf husband.

Michel de Montaigne, French essayist, 1533-1592
蒙田,法国散文家

❈ ❈ ❈ ❈ ❈ ❈

A great step toward independence is a good-humored stomach.

Lucius Annaeus Seneca, Roman philosopher, 4 BC? -65
塞尼卡,罗马哲学家

A woman is an occasional pleasure but a cigar is always a smoke.

Groucho Marx American comedian, 1895-1977
格劳索·马克斯,美国喜剧演员

As the births of living creatures are at first ill-shapen, so are all innovations, which are the births of time.

Francis Bacon, English philosopher, statesman, and essayist, 1561-1626
培根,英国哲学家、政治家、散文家

A lie can travel half way around the world while the truth is just putting on its shoes.

Mark Twain, American writer and humorist, 1835-1910
马克·吐温,美国作家、幽默家

A grave is a place where the dead are laid to await the coming of the medical student.

Ambrose Bierce, American writer of ghost stories, 1842-1914
比尔斯,美国作家

All rising to great place is by a winding stair.

Francis Bacon, English philosopher, statesman, and essayist, 1561-1626
培根,英国哲学家、政治家、散文家

And how is education supposed to make me feel smarter? Besides, every time I learn something new, it pushes some old stuff out of my brain. Remember when I took that home winemaking course, and I forgot how to drive?

Homer Simpson
辛普森

A bachelor's life is a fine breakfast, a flat lunch, and a miserable dinner.

Francis Bacon, English philosopher, statesman and essayist, 1561-1626
培根,英国哲学家、政治家、散文家

A banker is a fellow who lends you his umbrella when the sun is shining and wants it back the minute it begins to rain.

Mark Twain, American writer and humorist, 1835-1910
马克·吐温,美国作家、幽默家

❮❮❮❮❮❮❮❮❮❮

All things are cause for either laughter or weeping.

Lucius Annaeus Seneca, Roman philosopher
塞尼卡,罗马哲学家

❮❮❮❮❮❮❮❮❮

A LAUGH IS A SMILE THAT BURSTS.

Mary H. Waldrip
沃德利普

❮❮❮❮❮❮❮❮❮

A wise man will make more opportunities than he finds.

Francis Bacon, English philosopher, statesman and essayist,
1561-1626
培根,英国哲学家、政治家、散文家

❮❮❮❮❮❮❮❮❮

A good laugh is sunshine in a house.

William Makepeace Thackeray, British writer, 1811-1863
萨特雷,英国作家

*A*ge is an issue of mind over matter. If you don't mind, it doesn't matter.

Mark Twain, American writer and humorist, 1835-1910
马克·吐温，美国作家、幽默家

A sense of humor is a major defense against minor troubles.

Mignon McLaughlin
麦克劳林

*A*n idea isn't responsible for the people who believe in it.

Dan Marquis, American journalist and humorist, 1878-1937
丹·马奎斯，美国记者、幽默家

*A*n acquaintance is someone we know well enough to borrow from but not enough to lend to.

Ambrose Bierce, American writer of ghost stories, 1842-1914
比尔斯，美国作家

*A*s punishment for my contempt for authority, Fate has made me an authority myself.

Albert Einstein, American theoretical physicist, philosopher, 1875-1955
爱因斯坦，美国理论物理学家、哲学家

Beauty *itself is but the sensible image of the Infinite.*

Francis Bacon, English philosopher, statesman and essayist, 1561-1626

培根，英国哲学家、政治家、散文家

Beware of those who laugh at nothing or everything.

Arnold H. Glasgow

格拉斯哥

BUILDING castles in the air, and making yourself a laughing-stock.

Miguel de Cervantes, Spanish writer, 1547-1616

塞万提斯，西班牙作家

BY INDIGNITIES MEN COME TO DIGNITIES.

Francis Bacon, English philosopher, statesman and essayist, 1561-1626

培根，英国哲学家、政治家、散文家

Broadway is a street where people spend money they haven't earned to buy things they don't need to impress people they don't like.

Walter Winchell, American journalist, 1897-1972

温切尔，美国记者

9

Build a man a fire, and he'll be warm for a day. Set a man on fire, and he'll be warm for the rest of his life.

Terry Pratchett, British author
特里·普拉切特,英国作家

Boldness is ever blind, for it sees not dangers and inconveniences whence it is bad in council though good in execution.

Francis Bacon, English philosopher, statesman and essayist, 1561-1626
培根,英国哲学家、政治家、散文家

Comedy is tragedy that happens to other people.

Angela Carter, English journalist, 1940-1992
安杰拉·卡特,英国记者

Certainly the best works, and of greatest merit for the public, have proceeded from the unmarried, or childless men.

Francis Bacon, English philosopher, statesman and essayist, 1561-1626
培根,英国哲学家、政治家、散文家

Death and taxes and childbirth! There's never any convenient time for any of them.

Margaret Mitchell, American writer, 1900-1949
玛格丽特·米切尔,美国作家

DOGS LAUGH, BUT THEY LAUGH WITH THEIR TAILS.

Max Forrester Eastman, American writer and editor, 1883-1969
伊斯门,美国作家、编辑

Don't *wait to be happy to laugh... You may die and never have laughed!*

Jean LaBruyere, French writer, 1645-1696
拉布吕耶尔,法国作家

Doctors pours drugs of which they know little, to cure diseases of which they know less, into human beings of whom they know nothing.

Voltaire, French philosopher, 1604-1778
伏尔泰,法国哲学家

Do not *take life too seriously; you will never get out of it alive.*

Elbert Hubbard, American writer, 1856-1915
埃尔伯特·哈伯德,美国作家

Education is learning what you didn't even know you didn't know.

Daniel J. Boorstin, American historian
丹尼尔·布尔斯廷,美国当代历史学家

11

Experience is the name every one gives to their mistakes.

Oscar Wilde, Irish writer, playwright, 1854-1900
王尔德，爱尔兰作家、剧作家

Fame is like a river, that beareth up things light and swollen, and drowns things weighty and solid.

Francis Bacon, English philosopher, statesman,
and essayist, 1561-1626
培根，英国哲学家、政治家、散文家

From quiet homes and first beginning, out to the undiscovered ends, there's nothing worth the wear of winning, but laughter and the love of friends.

Hilaire Belloc, British writer, 1870-1953
贝洛克，英国作家

Fashion is only the attempt to realize art in living forms and social intercourse.

Francis Bacon, English philosopher, statesman and essayist, 1561-1626
培根，英国哲学家、政治家、散文家

Forgive, O Lord, my little jokes on Thee and I'll forgive Thy great big one on me.

Robert Frost, American poet, 1874-1963

弗罗斯特,美国诗人

For my name and memory I leave to men's charitable speeches, and to foreign nations and the next ages.

Francis Bacon, English philosopher, statesman and essayist, 1561-1626

培根,英国哲学家、政治家、散文家

From **your parents** you learn love and laughter and how to put one foot before the other. But when books are opened you discover that you have wings.

Helen Hayes, American actress, Academy Award winner

海斯,美国女演员、学院奖获得者

Fortune *is like the market, where, many times, if you can stay a little, the price will fall.*

Francis Bacon, English philosopher, statesman and essayist, 1561-1626

培根,英国哲学家、政治家、散文家

GOLF IS A GOOD WALK SPOILED.

Mark Twain, American writer and humorist, 1835-1910

马克·吐温,美国作家、幽默家

*G*ood fame is like fire; when you have kindled you may easily preserve it; but if you extinguish it, you will not easily kindle it again.

Francis! Bacon, English philosopher, statesman and essayist, 1561-1626

培根, 英国哲学家、政治家、散文家

HABIT IS A FORM OF EXERCISE.

Elbert Hubbard, American writer, 1856-1915

埃尔伯特·哈伯德, 美国作家

He that hath knowledge spareth his words.

Francis Bacon, English philosopher, statesman and essayist, 1561-1626

培根, 英国哲学家、政治家、散文家

*H*e who laughs last is generally the last to get the joke.

Terry Cohen

特里·科恩

He that will not apply new remedies must expect new evils; for time is the greatest innovator.

Francis Bacon, English philosopher, statesman and essayist, 1561-1626

培根, 英国哲学家、政治家、散文家

HE WHO LAUGHS, LASTS.

Mary Pettibone Poole
普尔

He who has achieved success has worked well, laughed often and loved much.

Elbert Hubbard, American writer, 1856-1915
埃尔伯特·哈伯特,美国作家

* * * * * *

He knows nothing, and he thinks he knows everything. That points clearly to a political career.

George Bernard Shaw, British playwright and critic, 1856-1950
萧伯纳,英国剧作家、批评家

Hope is a good breakfast, but it is a bad supper.

Francis Bacon, English philosopher, statesman and essayist, 1561-1626
培根,英国哲学家、政治家、散文家

I have found the best way to give advice to your children is to find out what they want, and then advise them to do it.

Harry S. Truman, American president, 1884-1972
杜鲁门,美国总统

I do not believe that any man fears to be dead, but only the stroke of death.

Francis Bacon, English philosopher, statesman
and essayist, 1561-1626
培根,英国哲学家、政治家、散文家

I hope that someday we will be able to put away our fears and prejudices and just laugh at people.

Jack Handey
汉迪

I will never be an old man. To me, old age is always *15* years older than I am.

Francis Bacon, English philosopher, statesman
and essayist, 1561-1626
培根,英国哲学家、政治家、散文家

I find television very educational. Every time someone switches it on, I go into another room and read a good book.

Groucho Marx, American comedian, actor and television
personality, 1895-1977
格劳菲奥·马克斯,美国喜剧演员、演员、电视人物

I CAN RESIST EVERYTHING EXCEPT TEMPTATION.

Oscar Wilde, Irish writer, playwright, 1854-1900
王尔德,爱尔兰作家、剧作家

If a manwill begin with certainties, he shall end in doubts, but if he will content to begin with doubts, he shall end in certainties.

Francis Bacon, English philosopher, statesman
and essayist, 1561-1626
培根,英国哲学家、政治家、散文家

☆ ☆ ☆ ☆ ☆ ☆

I have had a perfectly wonderful evening, but this wasn't it.

Woody Allen, American movie actor and director, 1935
伍迪·艾伦,美国电影演员、导演

If a man's wit be wandering, let him study the mathematics.

Francis Bacon, English philosopher, statesman
and essayist, 1561-1626
培根,英国哲学家、政治家、散文家

If you can't make it better, ***you can laugh at it***.

Erma Bombeck, American writer and humorist, 1927-1996

厄玛·邦贝克,美国作家、幽默家

If I had to live my life again, I'd make the same mistakes — only sooner.

Tallulah Bankfield, American actor, 1903-1965

塔卢拉·班克菲尔德,美国演员

It is *the ability to take a joke , not make one that proves you have a sense of humor .*

Max Forrester Eastman, American writer, editor, 1883-1969

伊斯门,美国作家、编辑

It takes a big man to cry, but it takes a bigger man to laugh at that man.

Jack Handey

杰克·汉迪

If we do not maintain justice , justice will not maintain us .

Francis Bacon, English philosopher, statesman
and essayist, 1561-1626

培根,英国哲学家、政治家、散文家

I used to always think that I'd look back on us crying and laugh, but I never thought I'd look back on us laughing and cry.

Ralph Waldo Emerson, American author, 1803-1882
爱默生,美国作家

If you're not allowed to laugh in heaven, I don't want to go there.

Martin Luther, German theologian, reformation leader, 1483-1546
马丁·路德,德国神学家、改革领袖

It was prettily devised of Aesop, "The fly sat on the axle tree of the chariot wheel and said, what dust do I raise!"

Francis Bacon, English philosopher, statesman and essayist, 1561-1626
培根,英国哲学家、政治家、散文家

I always divide people into two groups. Those who live by what they know to be a lie, and those who live by what whey believe, falsely, to be the truth.

Christopher Hampton, English playwright
克里斯托弗·汉普顿,英国当代剧作家

In peace, sons bury their fathers. In war, fathers bury their sons.

Herodotus, Greek historian, 5th century BC
希罗多德,希腊历史学家

If you try to fail and succeed, which have you done?

George Carlin, American comedian
卡林,美国喜剧演员

I figure you have the same chance of winning the lottery whether you play or not.

Fran Lebowitz, American journalist, 1951
弗兰·利博维兹,美国记者

It's not whether you win or lose, but how you place the blame.

Anonymous
佚名

If something's hard, then it's not worth doing.

Homer Simpson
辛普森

It is as natural to die as to be born; and to a little infant, perhaps, the one is as painful as the other.

Francis Bacon, English philosopher, statesman
and essayist, 1561-1626
培根,英国哲学家、政治家、散文家

It is inexcusable for scientists to torture animals; let them make their experiments on journalists and politicians.

Henrik Ibsen, Norwegian dramatist, 1828-1906
易卜生,挪威剧作家

If **you** can laugh together, you can work together.

Robert Orben, American humorist, speechwriter
罗伯特·奥尔本,美国幽默家、演讲作家

In times like these, it is helpful to remember that there have always been times like these.

Paul Harvey, American broadcaster
保罗·哈维,美国当代广播员

If you can't be a good example, then you'll just have to be a horrible warning.

Catherine Aird, British writer and artist
艾尔德,英国作家、艺术家

It is better to be beautiful than to be good. But... it is better to be good than to be ugly.

Oscar Wilde, Irish writer, playwright, 1854-1900
王尔德，爱尔兰作家、剧作家

If you haven't got anything nice to say about anybody, come and sit next to me.

Alice Roosevent Loongworth, American socialite
朗沃斯，美国社交名人

If you don't learn to laugh at trouble, you won't have anything to laugh at when you're old.

Edgar Watson Howe, American journalist, 1853-1937
豪，美国记者

I refuse to answer that question on the grounds that I don't know the answer.

Douglas Adams, English humorist & science fiction novelist, 1952-2001
道格拉斯·亚当斯，英国幽默家、科幻小说家

I have nothing to declare except my genius.

Oscar Wilde, Irish writer, playwright, 1854-1900
王尔德，爱尔兰作家、剧作家

I am free of all prejudices. I hate everyone e-qually.

W.C. Fields, American comedian actor, 1880-1946
费尔斯,美国喜剧演员

I hate music , especially when it's played .

Jimmy Durante, American jazz player, 1893-1980
吉米·杜兰特,美国爵士乐演奏家

IF IT SELLS , IT'S ART .

Frank Lloyd Wright, American architect, 1867-1959
弗兰克·莱特,美国建筑家

It's better to keep your mouth shut and appear stupid than to open it and remove all doubt.

Mark Twain, American writer and humorist, 1835-1910
马克·吐温,美国作家、幽默家

It is better to be hated for what you are than loved for what you are not.

Andre Gide, French writer, 1869-1951
纪德,法国作家

It's not that I'm afraid to die, I just don't want to be there when it happens.

Woody Allen, American movie actor, comedian, & director, 1935
伍迪·艾论,美国电影演员、喜剧演员、导演

In order for the light to shine so brightly, the darkness must be present.

Francis Bacon, English philosopher, statesman and essayist, 1561-1626
培根,英国哲学家、政治家、散文家

IT IS IMPOSSIBLE TO LOVE AND TO BE WISE.

Francis Bacon, English philosopher, statesman and essayist, 1561-1626
培根,英国哲学家、政治家、散文家

In taking revenge, a man is but even with his enemy; but in passing it over, he is superior.

Francis Bacon, English philosopher, statesman and essayist, 1561-1626
培根,英国哲学家、政治家、散文家

*J*ealousy is all the fun you think they had.

Erica Jong, American writer, 1917
雍,美国作家

*J*oyfulness keeps the heart and face young. A good laugh makes us better friends with ourselves and everybody around us.

Orison Swett Marden, 1850-1924
马顿

*L*augh and the world laughs with you. Snore and you sleep alone.

Anthony Burgess, British writer, critic
伯盖斯,英国作家、批评家

*L*ife is what happens to you while you're busy making other plans.

John Lennon, English Singer and songwriter, 1940-1980
约翰·列农,英国歌手、歌词作者

Last week I stated that this woman was the ugliest woman I had ever seen. I have since been visited by her sister and now wish to withdraw that statement.

Mark Twain, American writer and humorist, 1835-1910
马克·吐温,美国作家、幽默家

Lies are sufficient to breed opinion , and opinion brings on substance .

Francis Bacon, English philosopher, statesman and essayist, 1561-1626
培根,英国哲学家、政治家、散文家

Life lives, life dies. Life laughs, life cries. Life gives up and life tries. But life looks different through everyone's eyes.

Anonymous
佚名

*L*aughter is the best form of medicine. For when we laugh, we neither think, grieve, or feel.

Eugene Lam
拉姆

*L*ife, an age to the miserable, and a moment to the happy.

Francis Bacon, English philosopher, statesman and essayist, 1561-1626
培根, 英国哲学家、政治家、散文家

Laugh and the world laughs with you. Cry and the world laughs at you.

F. M. Linsner
林斯纳

Life doesn't imitate art, it imitates bad television.

Woody Allen, American movie actor, comedian, & director, 1935
伍迪·艾伦，美国电影演员、喜剧演员、导演

Love your neighbor; yet don't pull down your hedge

Benjamin Franklin, American statesman, diplomat and author 1706-1790
富兰克林，美国政治家、外交家、作家

Many a man's strength is in opposition, and when he faileth, he grows out of use.

Francis Bacon, English philosopher, statesman and essayist, 1561-1626
培根，英国哲学家、政治家、散文家

***Martyrdom*:** The only way a man can become famous without ability.

George Bernard Shaw, British playwright and critic, 1856-1950
萧伯纳，英国剧作家、批评家

Man has made use of his intelligence; he invented stupidity.

Remy de Gourmont, French novelist and philosopher, 1858-1915
古尔蒙，法国小说家、哲学家

MEN fear death as children fear to go in the dark and as that natural fear in children is increased by tales, so is the other.

Francis Bacon, English philosopher, statesman
and essayist, 1561-1626
培根,英国哲学家、政治家、散文家

Many of us spend half our time wishing for things we could have if we didn't spend half our time wishing.

Alexander Woollcott, American author and critic, 1887-1943
伍尔科特,美国作家、批评家

Marry me and I'll never look at another horse!

Groucho Marx, American comedian, 1895-1977
格劳索·马克斯,美国喜剧演员

Money is like manure, of very little use except it be spread.

Francis Bacon, English philosopher, statesman and essayist, 1561-1626
培根,英国哲学家、政治家、散文家

*M*an is the only animal that laughs and weeps; for he is the only animal that is struck with the difference between what things are, and what they ought to be.

William Hazlit, British essayist, 1778-1830

黑兹利特,英国散文家

*M*en are like a deck of cards. You'll find the occasional king, but most are jacks.

Laura Swenson

劳拉·斯温森

*M*odern art is what happens when painters stop looking at girls and persuade themselves they have a better idea.

John Ciardi, American poet and translator, 1916-1986

约翰·查尔迪,美国诗人、翻译家

*M*oney couldn't buy you friends, but you get a better class of enemy.

Spike Milligan, comic performers and writer

斯派克斯·米利根,滑稽演员、滑稽剧作者

May *the best day of your past be the worst day of your future.*

MAN PLANS AND GOD LAUGHS.

My interest is in the future because I am going to spend the rest of my life there.

My reputation grows with every failure.

Nothing doth more hurt in a state than that cunning men pass for wise.

Never go to a doctor whose office plants have died.

Erma Bombeck, American writer and humorist, 1927-1996
厄玛·邦贝克，美国作家、幽默家

NATURE IS COMMANDED BY OBEYING HER.

Francis Bacon, English philosopher, statesman and essayist, 1561-1626
培根，英国哲学家、政治家、散文家

Nothing shows a man's character more than what he laughs at.

Johann Wolfgang von Goethe, German writer, scientist, 1749-1832
歌德，德国作家、科学家

NOBODY EVER DIED OF LAUGHTER.

Max Beerbohm, British writer and caricaturist, 1872-1956
比尔博姆，英国作家、漫画家

Nature is often hidden, sometimes over-come, seldom extinguished.

Francis Bacon, English philosopher, statesmao and essayist, 1561-1626
培根，英国哲学家、政治家、散文家

Nothing is so useless as a general maxim.

Macaulay
麦考利

Next to power without honor, the most dangerous thing in the world is power without humor.

Eric Sevareid, American journalist, 1912-1992
塞瓦赖德,美国记者

Never keep up with the Joneses. Drag them down to your level. It's cheaper.

Quentin Crisp, British writer and actor, 1908-1999
克里斯普,英国作家、演员

Nothing is ever so bad that it can't get worse.

Gattuso
加图索

Nothing is more responsible for the good old days than a bad memory.

Franklin P. Adams, American writer and humorist, 1881-1960
弗兰克·亚当斯,美国作家、幽默家

Nothing so needs reforming as other people's habits.

Mark Twain, American writer and humorist, 1835-1910
马克·吐温, 美国作家、幽默家

Oh! Death will find me long before I tire of watching you.

Francis Bacon, British philosopher, statesman and essayist, 1561-1626
培根, 英国哲学家、政治家、散文家

Once you get people laughing, they're listening and you can tell them almost anything.

Herbert Gardner, American playwright, 1934-2003
加德纳, 美国剧作家

Opera in English is, in the main, just about as sensible as baseball in Italian.

H. L. Mencken, American editor, critic, 1880-1956
门肯, 美国编辑、批评家

OPPORTUNITY MAKES A THIEF.

Francis Bacon, Englishphilosopher, statesman and essayist, 1561-1626
培根, 英国哲学家、政治家、散文家

Of all the things I've lost, I miss my mind the most.

Mark Twain, American writer and humorist, 1835-1910
马克·吐温,美国作家、幽默家

Peace(n): In international affairs, a period of cheating between two periods of fighting.

Ambrose Bierce, American writer of ghost stories, 1842-1914
比尔斯,美国作家

Pictures and shapes are but secondary objects and please or displease only in the memory.

Francis Bacon, English philosopher, statesman and essayist, 1561-1626
培根,英国哲学家、政治家、散文家

Problems worthy of attack prove their worth by hitting back.

Piet Hein, Danish scientist and poet, 1905-1996
皮特·海因,丹麦科学家、诗人

People will sometimes forgive you the good you have done them, but seldom the harm they have done you.

W. Samerset Maugham, English writer, 1874-1965
毛姆,英国作家

*P*eople have discovered that they can fool the devil; but they can't fool the neighbors.

Francis Bacon, English philosopher, statesman
and essayist, 1561-1626
培根,英国哲学家、政治家、散文家

REAL PROBLEMS HAVE NO SOLUTIONS.

Anonymous
佚名

Remember, today is the tomorrow you worried about yesterday.

Dale Carnegie, American writer and speaker, 1888-1955
戴尔·卡耐基,美国作家、演说家

Reality is that which, when you stop believing it, doesn't go away.

Philip K. Dick, American writer, 1920-1982
菲利普·迪克,美国作家

Success produces success, just as money produces money.

Nicolas Chamfort, French journalist, playwright, 1741-1794
尚福尔,法国记者、剧作家

Seven days without laughter makes one weak.

Mort Walker, American comic artist
沃克,美国漫画家

Silence is the virtue of fools.

Francis Bacon, English philosopher, statesman and essayist, 1561-1626
培根,英国哲学家、政治家、散文家

So I went to the dentist. He said "Say Aaah." I said "Why?" He said "My dog's died."

Tommy Cooper, British comedians
汤米·库珀,英国喜剧演员

Some people are so dry that you might soak them in a joke for a month and it would not get through their skins.

Henry Ward Beecher, American clergyman, 1813-1887
比切,美国牧师

Someday they'll give a war and nobody will come.

Carl Sandburg, American poet and writer, 1874-1965
桑德堡,美国诗人、作家

The problem with political jokes is they get elected.

Henry Cate
凯特

The job of the artist is always to deepen the mystery.

Francis Bacon, British philosopher, statesman and essayist, 1561-1626
培根,英国哲学家、政治家、散文家

The person who can bring the spirit of laughter into a room is indeed blessed.

Bennett Alfred Cerf, American editor, publisher, 1898-1971
瑟夫,美国编辑、出版商

There are only two kinds of computer users: those who have lost data in a crash, and those who will lose data in a crash.

Bob LeVitus, American writer
鲍勃·勒维塔斯,美国当代作家

Truth is the daughter of time, not of authority.

Francis Bacon, British philosopher, statesman and essayist, 1561-1626
培根,英国哲学家、政治家、散文家

The human race has one really effective weapon and that is laughter.

Mark Twain, American author, humorist, 1835-1910
马克·吐温,美国作家、幽默家

The young man who has not wept is a savage, and the old man who will not laugh is a fool.

George Santayana, American philosopher, writer, 1863-1952
桑塔亚纳,美国哲学家、作家

The **difference** between a politician and statesman is: A politician thinks of the next election and a statesman thinks of the next generation.

James Freeman Clarke, American clergyman, 1810-1888
克拉克,美国牧师

To make mistakes is human; to stumble is commonplace; to be able to laugh at yourself is maturity.

William Arthur Ward, American scholar
沃德,美国学者

There is only one thing in life worse than being talked about, and that is not being talked about.

Oscar Wilde, Irish writer, playwright, 1854-1900
王尔德,爱尔兰作家、剧作家

The difference between the right word and the almost right word is the difference between lightning and a lightning bug.

Mark Twain, American writer and humorist, 1835-1910
马克·吐温, 美国作家、幽默家

The female of all species are most dangerous when they appear to retreat.

Dan Marquis, American journalist and humorist, 1878-1937
丹·马奎斯, 美国记者、幽默家

※ ※ ※ ※ ※ ※

There are three things men can do with women: love them, suffer for them, or turn them into literature.

Stephen Stills, American musician
史蒂芬·斯蒂尔斯, 美国音乐家

There are worse things in life than death. Have you ever spent an evening with an insurance salesman?

Groucho Marx American comedian, 1895-1977
格劳索·马克斯, 美国喜剧演员

There *are things known and there are things Anonymous, and in between are the doors.*

Jim Morrison, American singer, 1943-1971
吉姆·莫里森,美国歌手

To cease smoking *is the easiest thing. I ought to know. I've done it a thousand times.*

Mark Twain, American writer and humorist, 1835-1910
马克·吐温,美国作家、幽默家

The most wasted day of all is that on which we have not laughed.

Nicolas Chamfort, French journalist, playwright, 1741-1794
尚福尔,法国记者、剧作家

The **reward** for conformity is that everyone likes you except yourself.

Rita Mae Brown, American writer and poet
丽塔·梅·布朗,美国当代作家、诗人

*T*he best ideas come from jokes. Make your thinking as funny as possible.

David Ogilvie
奥格尔维

Trying is just the first step toward failure.

Homer Simpson
辛普森

The kind of humor I like is the thing that makes me laugh for *5* seconds and think for *10* minutes.

William Davis, American composer and bassoonist
威廉·戴维斯,美国作曲家、巴颂吹奏家

The brain is a wonderful organ; it starts working the moment you get up in the morning, and does not stop until you get into the office.

Robert Frost, American poet, 1874-1963
罗伯特·弗罗斯特,美国诗人

Three may keep a secret if two are dead.

Benjamin Franklin, American statesman, diplomat, 1706-1790
富兰克林,美国政治家、外交家

The world is full of willing people; some willing to work, the rest willing to let them.

Robert Frost, American poet, 1874-1963
弗罗斯特,美国诗人

The best way to cheer yourself is to cheer somebody else up.

Mark Twain, American writer and humorist, 1835-1910
马克·吐温,美国作家、幽默家

The real danger is not that computers will begin to think like men, but that men will begin to think like computers.

Sydney J. Harris, American journalist, 1917-1986
悉尼·哈里斯,美国记者

The information we have is not what we want.
The information we want is not what we need.
The information we need is not available.

Finagle's New Laws of Information, 1979
菲纳格尔,《信息新规则》

The past ain't what it used to be — it never was.

Anonymous
佚名

There is only one difference between a madman and me. I am not mad.

Salvador Dali, Spanish Surrealist Painter, 1904-1989
达里,西班牙超现实主义画家

*T*he reason that there are so few women comics is that so few women can bear being laughed at.

Anna Russell, British singer
安娜·罗素,英国歌手

*T*here are some things so serious you have to laugh at them.

Niels Henrik David Bohr, Danish physicist, chemist, 1885-1962
玻尔,丹麦物理学家、化学家

There are two kinds of statistics: the kind you look up and the kind you make up.

Rex Stout, American writer, 1886-1975
雷克斯·斯托特,美国作家

THE AIM OF a joke is not to degrade the human being but to remind him that he is already degraded.

George Orwell, British writer, 1903-1950
乔治·奥威尔,英国作家

To lose one parent may be regarded as a misfortune; to lose both looks like carelessness.

Oscar Wilde, Irish writer, playwright, 1854-1900
王尔德,爱尔兰作家、剧作家

The person who knows how to laugh at himself will never cease to be amused.

Shirley MacLaine, American actress
麦克莱恩,美国女演员

The man of understanding finds everything laughable.

Johann Wolfgang von Goethe, German writer, scientist, 1749-1832
歌德,德国作家、科学家

The blind man is laughing at the baldhead.

Persian Proverb
波斯谚语

The crisis of today is the joke of tomorrow.

Herbert George Wells, English author, 1866-1946
威尔斯,英国作家

The real wit tells jokes to make others feel superior, while the half-wit tells them to make others feel small.

Elmer Wheeler, American salesman
惠勒,美国推销员

Truth is always strange, stranger than fiction.

Francis Bacon, British philosopher, statesman and essayist, 1561-1626
培根,英国哲学家、政治家、散文家

Those who do not know how to weep with their whole hear don't know how to laugh either.

Golda Meir, prime minister of Israel, 1898-1978
迈尔,以色列总理

Whatever women do, they must do twice as well as men to be thought half as good. Luckily, this is not difficult.

Charlotte Whitton, Ottawa mayor, 1896-1975
夏洛特·惠顿,渥太华市长

Walking on water wasn't built in a day.

Jack Kerouac, American writer, 1992-1969
杰克·克洛克,美国作家

We are never so certain of our knowledge as when we're dead wrong.

Adair Lara, American journalist
阿代尔·拉拉,美国当代记者

When the mouse laughs at the cat there is a hole nearby.

Nigerian Proverb
尼日利亚谚语

We owe a lot to Thomas Edison. Were it not for him, we'd all be watching television by candlelight.

Milton Berle, American comedian, 1908-2002
米尔顿·伯利,美国喜剧演员

When did I realize I was God? Well, I was praying and I suddenly realized I was talking to myself.

Peter O'Toole, English actor
彼德·奥图尔,英国演员

When having my portrait painted I don't want justice, I want mercy.

Billy Hughes, Australia's prime minister, 1862-1952
比利·休斯,澳大利亚总理

When the fearful strain that is on me night and day, if I did not laugh I should die.

Abraham Lincoln, American President, 1809-1865
林肯,美国总统

When a stupid man is doing something he is ashamed of, he always declares that it is his duty.

George Bernard Shaw, British playwright and critic, 1856-1950

萧伯纳,英国剧作家、批评家

When people agree with me I always feel I must be wrong.

Oscar Wilde, Irish writer, playwright, 1854-1900

王尔德,爱尔兰作家、剧作家

When **we remember** we are all mad, the mysteries disappear and life stands explained.

Mark Twain, American writer and humorist, 1835-1910

马克·吐温,美国作家、幽默家

When **you are** down and out, something always turns up — and it's usually the noses of your friends.

Orson Welles, American writer, actor, and film director, 1915-1985

奥森·韦尔斯,美国作家、演员、电影导演

When a person can no longer laugh at himself, it is time for others to laugh at him.

Thomas S. Szasz, American psychiatrist

托马斯·萨兹,美国当代精神病学家

What I want to do is make people laugh so that they'll see things seriously.

William Zinsser, American writer, editor, and teacher
津瑟,美国作家、编辑、教师

Work is the curse of the drinking classes.

Oscar Wilde, Irish writer, playwright, 1854-1900
王尔德,爱尔兰作家、剧作家

We all know the rule of umbrellas — if you take your umbrella, it will not rain; if you leave it, it will.

Ralph Waldo Emerson, American philosopher, 1803-1882
爱默生,美国哲学家

Whenever I see an old lady slip and fall on a wet sidewalk, my first instinct is to laugh. But then I think, what if I was an ant, and she fell on me. Then it wouldn't seem quite so funny.

Jack Handey
汉迪

We read the world wrong and say that it deceives us.

Rabindranath Tagore, Indian poet, 1861-1941
泰戈尔,印度诗人

We must laugh at man, to avoid crying for him.

Napolean Bonaparte, French general, 1769-1821
拿破仑,法国将军

You can tell German wine from vinegar by the label.

Mark Twain, American writer and humorist, 1835-1910
马克·吐温,美国作家、幽默家

You don't stop laughing because you grow old; you grow old because you stop laughing.

Michael Pritchard
普里查德

You have to laugh at yourself because you'd cry your eyes out if you didn't.

Emily Saliers
萨利尔斯

You can no more win a war than you can win an earthquake.

Jeannette Rankin, Montana congresswoman, 1880-1973
珍妮特·兰金,美国蒙大拿州议员

You cannot hold back a good laugh any more than you can the tide. Both are forces of nature.

William Rotsler, cartoonist, 1926-1997
罗特斯勒,漫画家

You can't win at everything, but you can laugh at everything.

Robert Killinger
基林格

You grow up the day you have your first real laugh at yourself.

Ethel Barrymore, American actress, 1879-1959
巴里莫,美国演员

You can turn painful situations around through laughter. If you can find humor in anything -even poverty-you can survive it.

Bill Cosby, African-American comedian, author
比尔·考斯比,美国黑人喜剧演员、作家

Happiness

幸福

All I can say about life is, Oh God, enjoy it!

Bob Newhart, 1929-

鲍勃·纽哈特

Action may not always bring happiness; but there is no happiness without action.

Benjamin Disraeli, England's prime minister, 1804-1881

本杰明·迪斯雷利,英国首相

Act upon it, if you can!

Sir William S. Gilbert

吉尔伯特

A happy bridesmaid makes a happy bride.

Alfred, Lord Tennyson, British poet, 1809-1892

丁尼生,英国诗人

A *happy* woman is one who has no cares at all; a cheerful woman is one who has cares but doesn't let them get her down.

Beverly Sills, American writer, 1911-

西尔斯,美国作家

A man can be happy with any woman, as long as he does not love her.

Oscar Wilde, Irish writer, playwright, 1854-1900
王尔德, 爱尔兰作家、剧作家

A man is **happy** so long as he chooses to be happy and nothing can stop him.

Alexander Solzhenitsyn, Russian author, 1918-
索尔仁尼琴, 俄罗斯作家

A man of action forced into a state of thought is unhappy until he can get out of it.

John Galsworthy, British author, 1867-1933
高尔斯华绥, 英国作家

A person will be just about as happy as they make up their minds to be.

Abraham Lincoln, American president, 1809-1865
林肯, 美国总统

All truly great art is optimistic. The individual artist is happy in his creative work. The fact that practically all great art is tragic does not in any way change the above thesis。

Upton Sinclair, American novelist, 1878-1968
辛克莱, 美国小说家

A happy home is one in which each spouse grants the possibility that the other may be right, though neither believes it.

Don Fraser
弗雷泽

And because I am happy and dance and sing, They think they have done me no injury.

William Blake, British poet, artist, 1757-1827
布雷克,英国诗人、艺术家

All good men are happy when they choose to be their own authors. Those who choose to have others edit their pathways must live on the edge of another man's sword.

Julie Arabi
阿拉比

Ah! Happy years! Once more who would not be a boy?

George Gordon, British rebel, 1751-1793
乔治·戈顿,英格兰反叛者

All happy families resemble one another, but each unhappy family is unhappy in its own way.

Leo Tolstoy, Russian writer, philosopher, 1828-1910
托尔斯泰,俄罗斯作家、哲学家

A lifetime of happiness! No man alive could bear it: it would be hell on earth.

George Bernard Shaw, British playwright and critic, 1856-1950
萧伯纳,英国剧作家、批评家

Act happy, feel happy, be happy, without a reason in the world. Then you can love, and do what you will.

Dan Millman
米尔曼

A person is never happy except at the price of some ignorance.

Anatole France, French author, 1844-1924
法朗士,法国作家

A happy person is not a person in a certain set of circumstances, but rather a person with a certain set of attitudes.

Hugh Downs
唐斯

Associate with the noblest people you can find; read the best books; live with the mighty. But learn to be happy alone. Rely upon your own energies, and so do not wait for, or depend on other **people.**

Thomas Davidson
戴威森

A merry Christmas to everybody! A happy New Year to all the world!

Charles Dickens, English novelist, dramatist, 1812-1870

狄更斯,英国小说家、剧作家

Allow children to be ℏ𝕒𝕡𝕡𝕪 their own way; for what better way will they ever find?

Samuel Johnson, British author, 1709-1784

塞缪尔·约翰逊,英国作家

As a well-spent day brings happy sleep, so a life well spent brings *happy death*.

Leonardo da Vinci, Italian painter, 1452-1519

达芬奇,意大利画家

Be happy with what you have and are, be generous with both, and you won't have to hunt for happiness.

William Gladstone, British statesman and orator, 1809-1898

格莱斯顿,英国政治家、演说家

Be sober and temperate, and you will be healthy. Be in general virtuous, and you will be happy.

Benjamin Franklin, American statesman, diplomat, 1706-1790
富兰克林，美国政治家、外交家

*B*e virtuous and you'll be happy? Nonsense! Be happy and you'll begin to be virtuous.

James Gould Cozzens
科曾斯

Be happy while you're living, for you're a long time dead.

Scottish proverb
苏格兰谚语

Being happy is something you have to learn. I often surprise myself by saying "Wow, this is it." Guess I'm happy. I got a home I love. A career that I love. I'm even feeling more and more at peace with myself. If there's something else to happiness, let me know. I'm ambitious for that, too.

Harrison Ford
哈里森·福特

Call no man happy till he is dead.

Aeschylus, English lexicographer, critic, 1709-1784
埃斯库罗斯,英语辞典编纂家、批评家

Cherish all your **happy** moments; they make a fine cushion for old age.

Booth Tarkington, English lexicographer, critic, 1709-1784
塔金顿,英语辞典编纂家、批评家

Children aren't happy with nothing to ignore, and that's what parents were created for.

Ogden Nash, American poet, 1902-1971
纳什,美国诗人

Common sense and a sense of humor are the same thing, moving at different speeds. A sense of humor is just common sense.

Clive James
詹姆斯

Celebrate the happiness that friends are always giving; make every day a holiday and celebrate *just living*.

Amanda Bradley
阿尔曼达·布兰德利

Did you know... that when you walk past a flower, whether it be in somebody's garden or on a vacant hillside, the flower will always smile at you. The most polite way to respond, I've been told, is to cheerfully return the smile.

Ron Atchison
艾奇逊

Did you ever see an unhappy horse? Did you ever see bird that had the blues? One reason why birds and horses are not unhappy is because they are not trying to impress other birds and horses.

Dale Carnegie, American writer and speaker, 1888-1955
戴尔·卡耐基, 美国作家、演说家

Every gift from a friend is a wish for your happiness.

Richard Bach
理查德·巴赫

Each of us owes it to our spouse, our children, and our friends, to be as happy as we can be. And if you don't believe me, ask a child what it's like to grow up with an unhappy parent, or ask parents what they suffer if they have an unhappy child.

Dennis Prager
普拉格

Eating is not merely a material pleasure. Eating well gives a spectacular joy to life and contributes immensely to goodwill and happy companionship. It is of great importance to the morale.

Elsa Schiaparelli, Italian-French designer, 1890-1973
斯基帕雷利,法国设计师

Every body about me seems happy but every body seems in a hurry to be happy somewhere else.

Hannah Cowley, English playwright, 1743-1809
考利,英国剧作家

Every man is thoroughly happy twice in his life; just after he met his first love, and just after he has left his last one.

H. L. Mencken, American editor, satirist, 1880-1956
门肯,美国编辑、讽刺家

Follow thy fair sun, **unhappy** shadow.

Thomas Campion
坎皮恩

Frankly, I think the chances of having a happy childhood

while you're still a kid *going* through it are pretty slim.

Edith Ann, American actress/comedian
伊迪丝·安,美国女演员

For in all adversity of fortune the worst sort of misery is to have been happy.

Boethius, Roman philosopher
波伊提乌,罗马哲学家

Good humor is one of the best articles of dress one can wear in society.

William Makepeace Thackeray, British writer, 1811-63
萨特雷,英国作家

Grief can take care of itself, but to get the full value of a joy you must have somebody to divide it with.

Mark Twain, American writer and humorist, 1835-1910
马克·吐温,美国作家、幽默家

Goodness does not more certainly make men happy than happiness makes them good.

Walter Savage Landor, British author, 1775-1864
沃尔特·兰多,英国作家

Growing up is not being so dead-set on making *every-body happy.*

Reba McEntire, American country singer, 1954 -
麦肯泰尔,美国乡村音乐歌手

Happiness was not made to be boasted, but enjoyed. Therefore tho' others count me miserable, I will not believe them if I know and feel myself to be happy; nor fear them.

Thomas Traherne, English poet, mystic, 1637-1674 ·
特拉赫恩

Happiness walks on busy feet.

Kitte Turmell
特梅尔

Happiness is a Swedish sunset; it is there for all, but most of us look the other way and lose it.

Mark Twain, American writer and humorist, 1835-1910
马克·吐温,美国作家、幽默家

Happiness is a conscious choice, not an automatic response.

Mildred Barthel
米尔德里德·巴塞尔

Happiness is perfume; you can't pour it on somebody else without getting a few drops on yourself.

James Van Der Zee
詹姆斯·齐

Happiness consists more in small conveniences or pleasures that occur every day, than in great pieces of good fortune that happen but seldom to a man in the course of his life.

Benjamin Franklin, American statesman, diplomat, 1706-1790
富兰克林,美国政治家、外交家

Happiness makes up in height for what it lacks in length.

Robert Frost, American poet, 1874-1963
弗罗斯特,美国诗人

Happiness is not a destination. It is a method of life.

Burton Hills
希尔斯

Happiness in the present is only shattered by comparison with the past.

Dough Horton
霍顿

Happiness is liberty from everything that makes us unhappy.

Vernon Howard
霍华德

Happiness is the only good. The time to be happy is now. The place to be happy is here. The way to be happy is to make others so.

Robert Green Ingersoll, American statesman and public spenker, 1833-1899
英格索尔,美国政治家、演讲家

Happiness is an attitude of mind, born of the simple determination to be happy under all outward circumstances.

J. Donald Walters
沃尔特

Happiness is something that comes into our lives through doors we don't even remember leaving open.

Rose Lane
莱恩

Happiness isn't something you experience; it's something you remember.

Oscar Levant, 1906-1972
黎凡特

Happiness is inward, and not outward; and so, it does not depend on what we have, but on what we are.

Henry Van Dyke
戴克

65

Happiness is not having what you want, but wanting what *you have*.

Rabbi H. Schachter
沙赫特

He who laughs last didn't get it.

Helen Giangregorio
吉安格利格里奥

He who laughs last has not yet heard the bad news.

Bertolt Brecht
布雷赫特

Happiness is always a by-product. It is probably a matter of temperament, and for anything I know it may be glandular. **But** it is not something that can be demanded from life, and if you are not happy you had better stop worrying about it and see what treasures you can pluck from your own brand of *unhappiness*.

Robertson Davies
戴威斯

Happiness is a thing to be practiced, like the violin.

John Lubbock, British banker, politician and naturalist, 1834-1913
卢伯克,英国银行家,政治家,博物学家

Happiness is not something you postpone for the future; it is something you design for the present.

Jim Rohn
罗恩

Happy people plan actions, they don't plan results.

Dennis Wholey
沃利

Happiness lies in the joy of achievement and the thrill of creative effort.

Franklin D. Roosevelt, American president, 1882-1945
富兰克林·罗斯福,美国总统

Happiness is nothing more than good health and a bad memory.

Albert Schweitzer, German physician and theologian, 1875-1965
施韦策,德国医生、神学家

Happiness comes of the capacity to *feel* deeply, to enjoy simply, to think freely, to risk life, to be needed.

Storm Jameson
詹姆森

Happiness is not a reward-it is a consequence. Suffering is not a punishment-it is a result.

Robert Green Ingersoll, American statesman and public speaker, 1833-1899
英格索尔,美国政治家,演讲家

Hope is itself a species of happiness, and, perhaps, the chief happiness which this world affords.

Samuel Johnson, English author, 1709-1784
塞缪尔·约翰逊,英国作家

Happiness is having a large, loving, caring, close-knit family in another *city*.

George Burns, American comedian, 1896-1996
乔治·彭斯,美国喜剧演员

Happy is the nation without a history.

Marchese di Beccaria Cesare
西泽里

Happiness: *a good* bank account, a good cook and a good digestion.

Jean Jacques Rousseau, French author and philosopher, 1712-1778
卢梭,法国作家、哲学家

Happiness is that state of consciousness which proceeds from the achievement of one's values.

Ayn Rand, American author, 1905-1982
兰德,美国作家

Happiness is neither virtue nor pleasure nor this thing nor that but simply growth. We are happy when we are growing.

William Butler Yeats, Irish writer, 1865-1939
叶芝,爱尔兰作家

I were but little happy, if I could say how much.

William Shakespeare, English playwright and poet, 1564-1616
莎士比亚,英国剧作家、诗人

It is the mind that makes good or ill,
that makes wretch or happy, rich or poor.

Edmund Spencer
斯宾塞

It is an unhappy **lost** that finds no enemies.

Maxims
马克西姆斯

*T*hose who are unhappy have no need for anything in this world but people capable of giving them their attention.

Simone Weil
威尔

It is pretty hard to tell what does bring happiness; poverty and wealth have both failed.

Kin Hubbard, 1868-1930
金·哈伯特

It is by not always thinking of **yourself**, if you can manage it, that you might somehow be happy. Until you make room in your life for someone as important to you as yourself, you will always be searching and lost ...

Richard Bach, American novelist, author, 1936 -
巴赫，美国小说家、作家

I've grown to realize the joy that comes from little victories is preferable to the fun that comes from ease and the pursuit of pleasure.

Lawana Blackwell
拉瓦拉·布莱克韦尔

If you are not happy here and now, you never will be.

Taisen Deshimaru
德什马鲁

If there were in the world today any large number of people who desired their own happiness more than they desired the unhappiness of others, we could have paradise in a few years.

Bertrand Russell, British philosopher, 1872-1970
罗素,英国哲学家

If you're trying to remember a happy memory, don't think back to a time when you were ALSO thinking of a happy memory, because man, how long does this **go on**?

Jack Handey
汉迪

If two people *love* each other, there can be no happy end to it.

Ernest Hemingway, American writer, 1899-1961

海明威,美国作家

I have no **money**, no resources, no hopes. I am the happiest man alive.

Henry Miller, American author, 1891-1980

亨利·米勒,美国作家

It is not how much we have, but how much we enjoy, that makes *happiness*.

Charles Haddon Spurgeon

斯珀吉翁

It is happy for you that you possess the talent of flattering with delicacy. May I ask whether these pleasing attentions proceed from the impulse of the moment, or are the result of previous **study**?

Jane Austen, British author, 1775-1817

奥斯丁,英国作家

In order to have great happiness, you have to have great pain and unhappiness-otherwise how would you know when you're happy?

Leslie Caron
莱斯利·卡伦

I cannot even imagine where I would be today were it not for that handful of friends who have given me a heart full of joy. Let's face it, friends make life a lot more fun。,

Charles R. Swindoll
斯温朵尔

I've learned from experience that the greater part of our happiness or misery depends on our dispositions and not on our circumstances.

Martha Washington, wife of George Washington, 1731-1802
马莎·华盛顿,乔治·华盛顿之妻

In order for people to be happy, sometimes they have to take risks. It's true these risks can put them in danger of being *hurt*.

Meg Cabot
卡柏

73

I *don't know* what your destiny will be, but one thing I do know: the only ones among you who will be really happy are those who have sought and found how to serve.

Albert Schweitzer, German physician and theologian, 1875-1965
施韦策, 德国医生、神学家

I am ignorant and impotent and yet, somehow or other, here I am **unhappy**, no doubt, profoundly dissatisfied... In spite of everything I survive.

Aldous Huxley
赫胥黎

If only we'd stop trying to be happy we could have a pretty good time.

Edith Newbold Jones Wharton, American writer, 1862-1937
奥顿, 美国作家

It is better to be happy for a moment and be burned up with beauty than to live a long time and be bored all the while.

Helen Keller, American author and lecturer, 1880-1968
海伦·凯勒, 美国作家、演讲家

It isn't what you have, or who you are, or where you are, or what you are doing that makes you happy or unhappy. It is what you think about.

Dale Carnegie, American writer and speaker, 1888-1955
戴尔·卡耐基,美国作家、演说家

I think it a·very happy accident.

Miguel de Cervantes, Spanish writer, 1547-1616
塞万提斯,西班牙作家

If you want anything done well, do it yourself. This is why *most people* laugh at their own jokes.

Bob Edwards
鲍勃·爱德华斯

Indeed, man wishes to be happy even when he so lives as to make happiness impossible.

Saint Augustine, Christian church father, philosopher, 354-430
奥古斯丁,基督教创始人、哲学家

It's never too late to have a **happy** childhood.

Wayne Dyer, American writer, 1940
戴尔,美国作家

75

If you want to live a happy life, tie it to a goal. Not to people or things.

Albert Einstein, American theoretical physicist, philosopher, 1875-1955
爱因斯坦,美国理论物理学家、哲学家

Job was **not** so miserable in his sufferings, as happy in his patience.

Thomas Fuller, English clergyman and historian, 1608-1661
托马斯·富勒,英国牧师、历史学家

Joy comes from using your potential.

Will Schultz
舒尔茨

Joy is not in things; it is in us.

Richard Wagner, German composer, 1813-1883
里查德·瓦格纳,德国作曲家

Learn to be calm and you will *always* be happy.

Paramhansa Yogananda
尤伽南达

Little deeds of kindness, little words of love, help to make earth happy like the heaven above.

Julia A. Fletcher Carney
卡尼

Learn to laugh at your troubles and you'll never run out of things to laugh at.

Lyn Karol
卡洛尔

Love is seeking to make another person happy.

Anonymous
佚名

Let us all be happy and live within our means, even if we have to borrow the money to do it with.

Charles Farrar Browne
布朗

Let us be grateful to **people** who make us happy; they are the charming gardeners who make our souls blossom.

Marcel Proust, French writer, 1871-1922
普鲁斯特,法国作家

Learning to live in the present moment is part of the path of joy.

Sarah Ban Breathnach

布雷斯纳奇

Let *him* who would enjoy a good future waste none of his present.

Roger Babson

巴布森

Money doesn't make you happy. I now have $50 million but I was just as happy when I had $48 million.

Arnold Schwarzenegger, American actor, governor

阿诺·施瓦辛格,美国电影演员、州长

Men can only be happy when they do not assume that the object of life is happiness.

George Orwell, British author, 1903-1950

乔治·奥维尔,英国作家

My happiness derives from knowing the people I love are *happy*.

Holly Ketchel

霍利·凯查尔

Most people would rather be certain they're miserable, than risk being happy.

Robert Anthony
罗伯特·安东尼

My love does not, cannot make her happy. My love can only release in her the capacity to **be happy.**

J. Barnes
巴恩斯

Money never made a man happy yet, nor will it. There is nothing in its nature to produce happiness. The more a man has, the more he wants. Instead of filling a vacuum, it makes one.

Benjamin Franklin, American statesman, diplomat, 1706-1790
富兰克林,美国政治家、外交家

Make happy those who are near, and those who are far will come.

Chinese proverb
中国谚语

May your walls know joy; May every room hold laughter and every window open to great possibility.

Maryanne Radmacher-Hershey
拉德马赫荷尔希

No man can **be happy** without a friend, nor be sure of his friend till he is unhappy.

Francis Scott Fitzgerald , American writer , 1896-1940
菲茨杰尔德,美国作家

No-one is completely unhappy at the failure of his best **friend**.

Groucho Marx , American comedian , 1895-1977
格劳索·马克斯,美国喜剧演员

No man chooses evil **because** it is evil; he only mistakes it for happiness.

Mary Wollstonecraft
沃尔斯通克拉夫特

Now is the time for *all good* men to come to.

Walt Kelly , American cartoonist , 1913-1973
凯利,美国漫画家

Only when a man's life comes to its end in prosperity dare we pronounce him happy.

Aeschylus, English lexicographer, critic, 1709-1784

埃斯库罗斯,英语辞典学家、批评家

Only two things are necessary to keep one's wife happy. One is to let her think she is having her own way, and the other is to let her have it.

Lyndon B. Johnson, American president, 1908-1973

约翰逊,美国总统

One must laugh before one is happy, or one may die without ever laughing at all.

Jean de La Bruy

琼·德拉布鲁

People take different roads seeking fulfillment and happiness. Just because they're not on your road doesn't mean they've gotten lost.

H. Jackson Browne

杰克逊·布朗

Poetry is the record of the best and happiest moments of the happiest and best minds.

Percy Bysshe Shelley, British poet, 1792-1822

雪莱,英国诗人

81

People who've had happy childhoods are wonderful, but they're bland... An unhappy childhood compels you to use your imagination to create a world in which you can be happy. Use your old grief. That's the gift you're given.

Baron Patrick Maynard Stuart, British physicist, 1897-1974
斯图尔特,英国物理学家

Parents were invented to make children happy by giving them something to ignore.

Ogden Nash, American writer, 1902-1971
纳什,美国作家

Real happiness is when you marry a girl for love and find out later she has money.

Bob Monkhouse, British comedian and television host, 1928-2003
鲍勃·蒙克豪斯,英国喜剧演员、电视主持人

Remember that as a teenager you are at the last stage in your life when you will be happy to hear that the phone is for *you*.

Fran Lebowitz, American journalist, 1951-
弗兰·利博维兹,美国记者

Remember this that very little is needed to make a happy life.

Marcus Aurelius Antoninus , Roman Emperor, 121-180
安东尼努斯,罗马皇帝

Realize that true happiness lies within *you*. Waste no time and effort searching for peace and contentment and joy in the world outside. Remember that there is no happiness in having or in getting, but only in giving. Reach out. Share. Smile. Hug.

Og Mandino
曼迪诺

Real joy comes not *from* ease or riches or from the praise of men, but from doing something worthwhile.

Sir Wilfred Grenfell, British missionary and physician, 1865-1940
格伦费尔,英国传道士、医生

Remember that happiness is a way of travel, not a destination.

Roy Goodman
古德曼

Rest is not idleness, and to lie sometimes on the grass on a summer day listening to the murmur of water, or watching the clouds float across the sky, is hardly a waste of time.

John Lubbock, British banker, politician, and naturalist
卢伯克,英国银行家、政治家、博物学家

Some cause happiness wherever they go; others whenever they go.

Oscar Wilde, Irish writer, playwright, 1854-1900
王尔德,爱尔兰作家、剧作家

Success is getting what you want, happiness is wanting what you **get.**

Dave Gardner
加德纳

Sometimes we are less unhappy in being deceived by those we love, than in being undeceived by them.

Fran
弗兰

Sometimes it is a great joy just to listen to someone we love talking.

Vincent McNabb
麦克纳伯

Sometimes it's hard to avoid the happiness of others.

David Assael
阿萨尔

The pursuit of happiness is a most ridiculous phrase; if you pursue happiness you'll never find it.

C. P. Snow, British novelist, 1905-1980
斯诺,美国小说家

The **greatest happiness** of life is the conviction that we are loved-loved for ourselves, or rather, loved in spite of ourselves.

Victor Hugo, French poet, dramatist and novelist, 1802-1885
雨果,法国诗人、剧作家、小说家

The only joy in the world is to begin.

Cesare Pavese, Italian poet, critic, novelist and translator, 1908-1950
帕韦泽,意大利诗人、评论家、小说家、翻译家

There is no greater joy nor greater reward than to make a fundamental difference in someone's life.

Sister Mary Rose McGeady
麦克吉迪

The more refined one is, the unhappier.

Anton Chekhov, Russian author, 1860-1904
契珂夫,俄罗斯作家

To be happy one must have a good stomach and a bad

heart.

Bernard de Fontenelle
丰特奈尔

That is the best-to laugh with someone because you think the same things are funny.

Gloria Vanderbilt
范德比尔特

To be interested in the changing seasons is a happier state of mind than to be hopelessly in love with spring.

George Santayana, American educator, philosopher and poet, 1863-1952
桑塔亚纳,美国教育家、哲学家、诗人

The **happiness** of a man in this life does not consist in the absence but in the mastery of his passions.

Alfred Lord Tennyson, British poet, 1809-1892
丁尼生,英国诗人

The surest way to happiness is to lose **yourself** in a cause greater than yourself.

Anonymous
佚名

To attain happiness in another world we need only to believe something; to secure it in this world, we must do something.

Charlotte Perkins Gilman, American reformer and author, 1860-1935
吉尔曼，美国改革家、作家

The happy man is not he who seems thus to others, but who seems thus to *himself*.

Marcel Proust, French writer, 1871-1922
普鲁斯特，法国作家

The happiest people seem to be those who have no particular cause for being happy except that they are so.

William Ralph Inge, British writer, 1860-1954
威廉·拉尔夫·英，英国作家

There are as many nights as days, and the one is just as long as the other in the year's course. Even a happy life cannot be without a measure of darkness, and the word "*happy*" would lose its meaning if it were not balanced by sadness.

Carl Gustav Jung, Swiss psychiatrist, founded psychology, 1875-1961
荣格,瑞士心理学家、心理学创始人

The secret of happiness is to make others believe they are the cause of it.

Al Batt
阿尔·巴特

To be happy, we must be true to nature and carry our age along with *us*.

William Hazlit, British essayist, 1778-1830
黑兹利特,英国散文家

The foolish man seeks happiness in the distance, the wise grows it under his **feet**.

James Oppenheim
欧佩海姆

The pleasantest things in the **world** are pleasant thoughts; and the great art of life is to have as many of them as possible.

Michel de Montaigne, French essayist , 1533-1592
蒙田，法国散文家

The only truly happy people are children and the creative minority.

Jean Caldwell
考德威尔

There is no way to be completely happy without being oblivious to the world around you.

Maredith Close
马雷迪斯·克洛斯

The real test of friendship is: can you literally do *noth-ing* with the other person? Can you enjoy those moments of life that are utterly simple?

Eugene Kennedy
肯尼迪

The bond that links your true **family** is not one of blood, but of respect and joy in each other's life. Rarely do members of one family grow up under the same roof.

Richard Bach
里查德·巴赫

The only way to be happy is to love to suffer.

Woody Allen, American movie actor, director, 1935-
伍迪·艾伦,美国电影演员、导演

There are hundreds of languages in the world, but a smile speaks *them all*.

Anonymous
佚名

There is in the worst of fortune the best of chances for a **happy** change.

Euripidese, Greek dramatist, 480-406 B.C.
欧里庇得斯,希腊剧作家

The secret of happiness is not in doing what one likes, but in liking what one does.

James M. Barrie, Scottish author, 1860-1937
詹姆斯·巴里,苏格兰作家

The secret of happiness is something to do.

John Burroughs, American naturalist and author, 1837-1921
约翰·伯勒，美国博物学家、作家

The grand essentials of happiness are: something to do, something to love, and something to hope for.

Allan K. Chambers
艾伦·钱伯斯

The human spirit needs to accomplish, to achieve, to triumph to be *happy*.

Ben Stein
本·斯坦

The happy person is the one who finds occasions for joy at every step. He does not have to look for them; he just finds them.

Ossian Lang
兰

To have **joy** one must share it. Happiness was born a twin.

Lord Byron, English poet, 1788-1824
拜伦，英国诗人

The majority of men devote the greater part of their lives to making their remaining years unhappy.

Jean de La Bruy
琼·德拉布鲁

To be truly happy is a *question* of how we begin and not of how we end, of what we want and not of what we have.

Robert Louis Balfour Stevenson, British writer, 1850-1894
史蒂文森,英国作家

The discovery of a new dish does more for human **happiness** than the discovery of a new star.

Anthelme Brillat-Savarin, French politician and gourmet, 1755-1826
布里亚-萨瓦尔,法国政治家、美食家

Unhappiness is not knowing what we want and killing ourselves to get it.

Don Herold
赫罗尔德

We act as though comfort and luxury were the chief requirements of life, when all that we need to make us really happy is something to be enthusiastic about.

Charles Kingsley
查尔斯·金斯利

We are at our very best, and we are **happiest**, when we are fully engaged in work we enjoy on the journey toward the goal we've established for ourselves. It gives meaning to our time off and comfort to our sleep. It makes everything else in life so wonderful, so worthwhile.

Earl Nightingale, British nursing pioneer, 1820-1910
南丁格尔,英国护理先驱

We don't make mistakes here; we just have happy accidents. From the Joy of *Painting*.

Bob Ross
鲍勃·罗斯

Winning is important to me, but what brings me real joy is the experience of being fully engaged in whatever I'm *doing*.

Phil Jackson
菲尔·杰克逊

We take greater pains to persuade others that we are happy than in endeavoring to think so **ourselves.**

Confucius, Chinese philosopher and educator
孔子,中国哲学家、教育家

When you were born, you cried and the world rejoiced. Live your life so that when you die, the world cries and you rejoice.

Cherokee Expression
切罗基人谚语

Who will tell whether one happy moment of love, or the joy of breathing or walking on a bright morning and smelling the fresh air, is not worth all the suffering and effort which life implies?

Erich Fromm, German psychoanalyst and social theorist, 1900-1980
艾里克·弗罗姆,德国心理分析家、社会理论家

We find greatest joy, not in ｇｅｔｔｉｎｇ, but in expressing what we are...Men do not really live for honors or for pay; their gladness is not the taking and holding, but in doing, the striving, the building, the living. It is a higher joy to teach than to be taught. It is good to get justice, but better to do it.

R. J. Baughan
鲍恩

What's the use of happiness? It can't buy you *money*.

Henny Youngman
扬曼

We tend to forget that happiness doesn't come as a result of getting something we don't have, but rather of recognizing and appreciating what we do *have*.

Fredrick Koeing
凯因

We are convinced that happiness is never to be found, and each believes it is possessed by others, to keep alive the hope of obtaining it for himself.

Samuel Johnson, British author and lexicographer, 1709-1784
塞缪尔·约翰逊,英国作家、词典编纂家

We *could* never learn to be brave and patient, if there were only joy in the world.

Helen Keller, American author and lecturer, 1880-1968
海伦·凯勒,美国作家、演讲家

We cannot be contented because we are happy, and we cannot be happy because we are *contented*.

Walter Savage Landor, English author, 1775-1864
沃尔特·兰多

When one door of happiness closes, another opens; but often we look so long at the closed door that we do not see the one which has opened for us.

Helen Keller, American author and lecturer, 1880-1968
海伦·凯勒，美国作家、演讲家

We're constantly striving for success, fame and comfort when all we really need to be happy is someone or some thing to be enthusiastic about.

H. Jackson Brown, Jr.
布朗

Work joyfully and peacefully, knowing that right thoughts and right efforts inevitably bring about right results.

James Allen
詹姆斯·艾伦

What counts in making a happy marriage is not so much how compatible you are, but how you deal with incompatibility.

George Levinger
莱文杰

We are not the same persons this year as last; nor are those we love. It is a happy chance if we, changing, continue to love a changed person.

Jacques Maritain, French philosopher, critic, 1882-1973
马利丹，法国哲学家、批评家

We choose our joys and sorrows long before we experience *them*.

Kahlil Gibran, Lebanon poet, philosopher and artist, 1883-1931
纪伯伦,黎巴嫩诗人、哲学家、艺术家

Wisdom is the supreme part of happiness.

Sophocles, Greek dramatist, 496-406 B.C.
索福克勒斯,希腊剧作家

*W*e are no longer happy as soon as we wish to be happier.

Walter Savage Landor, English author, 1775-1864
沃尔特·兰多,英国作家

We all live with the objective of being happy; our lives are all different and yet the same.

Anne Frank
弗兰克

You will never be happy if you continue to search for what happiness consists of. You will never live if you are looking for the meaning of life.

Albert Camus, French author, 1913-1960
加缪,法国作家

$\mathcal{Y}$ou won't be happy with more until you're happy with what you've got.

Angel Blessing
布莱辛

You cannot be healthy; you cannot be happy; you cannot be prosperous, if you have a bad disposition.

Emmet Fox
福克斯

Inspiration

灵感

An inventor is simply a fellow who doesn't take his education too seriously.

Charles. Kettering, American inventor, 1876-1958
凯特林,美国发明家

Any man who is under 30, and is not a liberal, has not heart; and any man who is over 30, and is not a conservative, has no brains.

Sir Winston Churchill, British Prime Minister, 1874-1965
丘吉尔,英国首相

A little inaccuracy sometimes saves a ton of explanation.

H. H. Munro (Saki), British author, 1870-1916
芒罗,英国作家

A MAN CAN'T BE TOO CAREFUL IN THE CHOICE OF HIS ENEMISE.

Oscar Wilde, Irish writer and playwright, 1854-1900
王尔德,爱尔兰作家、剧作家

A friendship founded on business is better than a business founded on friendship.

John D. Rockefeller, American philanthropist, 1874-1960
洛克菲勒,美国慈善家

A person that values its privileges above its principles soon loses both.

Dwight D. Eisenhower, American president, 1890-1969
艾森豪威尔,美国总统

Argue for your limitations, and sure enough they're yours.

Richard Bach
巴赫

A witty saying proves nothing.

Voltaire, French philosopher, 1604-1778
伏尔泰,法国哲学家

All truth passes through three stages. First, it is ridiculed. Second, it is violently opposed. Third, it is accepted as being self-evident.

Arthur Schopenhauer, German philosopher, 1788-1860
叔本华,德国哲学家

Anything that is *too* stupid to be spoken is sung.

Voltaire, French philosopher, 1604-1778

伏尔泰，法国哲学家

Always do right — this will gratify some and astonish the rest.

Mark Twain, American writer and humorist, 1835-1910

马克·吐温，美国作家、幽默家

Ask her to wait a moment — I am almost done.

Carl Friedrich Gauss, German mathematician and astronomer,
while working, when informed that his wife is dying

高斯，德国数学家、天文学家

A pessimist sees the difficulty in every opportunity; an optimist sees the opportunity in every difficulty.

Sir Winston Churchill, British Prime Minister, 1874-1965

丘吉尔，英国首相

A husband is what is left of the lover after the nerve has been extracted.

Helen Rowland, 1876-1950
罗兰

A SCHOLAR WHO cherishes the love of comfort is not fit to be deemed a scholar.

Lao Zi, *Chinese philosopher*
老子,中国哲学家

$\mathcal{A}$ poem is never finished, only abandoned.

Paul Valery, *French poet*, 1871-1945
瓦莱里,法国诗人

Being on the tightrope is living; everything else is waiting.

Karl Wallenda
瓦伦达

Behind every great fortune there is a crime.

Honore de Balzac, *French author*, 1799-1850
巴尔扎克,法国作家

BE NICE TO PEOPLE on your way up because you meet them on your way down.

Jimmy Durante, American jazz player, 1893-1980
吉米·杜兰特,美国爵士乐演奏家

Basically, I no longer work for anything but the sensation I have while *working* .

Albert Giacometti, Swiss sculptor and painter
贾科米蒂,瑞士雕塑家、画家

Be glad of life, because it gives you the chance to love and to work and to play and to look up at the stars.

Henry Van Dyke, American author and clergyman
戴克,美国作家、牧师

Be not afraid of life. Believe that life is worth living, and your belief will help create the fact.

Willian James, American psychologist and philosopher, 1842-1910
威廉·詹姆斯,美国心理学家、哲学家

Convinced myself, *I* seek not to convince.

Edgar Allan Poe, American poet, 1809-1849
艾伦坡,美国诗人

Copy from one, it's plagiarism; copy from two, it's research.

Addison Mizner, American architect, 1876-1933
米泽纳,美国建筑家

Criticism is prejudice made plausible.

Henry Louis Mencken, American editor and critic, 1880-1956
门肯,美国编辑、批评家

Democracy does not guarantee equality of conditions-it only guarantees equality of opportunity.

Irving Kristol
克里斯托尔

Drag your thoughts away from your troubles... by the ears, by the heels, or any other way you can manage it.

Mark Twain, American writer and humorist, 1835-1910
马克·吐温,美国作家、幽默家

Do not accustom yourself to use big words for little matters.

Samuel Johnson, British author and lexicographer, 1709-1784
塞缪尔·约翰逊，英国作家，词典编纂家

Do, or do not. There is no 'try'.

Yoda
尤达

Don't stay in bed, unless you can make money in bed.

George Burns, American comedian, 1896-1996
乔治·彭斯，美国喜剧演员

Don't know why we are here, but I'm pretty sure that it is not in order to enjoy ourselves.

Ludwig Wittgenstein, Austrian philosopher, 1889-1951
维特根斯坦，奥地利哲学家

Don't be so humble — you are not that great.

Golda Meir, Prime Minister of Israel, 1898-1978
迈尔,以色列总理

Don't ask yourself what the world needs; ask yourself what makes you come alive. And then go and do that. Because what the world needs is people who have come alive.

Harold Whitman, American poet
惠特曼,美国诗人

Do oot go where the path may lead, go instead where there is no path and leave a trail.

Ralph Waldo Emerson, American author, 1803-1882
爱默生,美国作家

Everything has been figured out, except how to live.

Jean-Paul Sartre, French author and philosopher, 1905-1980
萨特,法国作家、哲学家

Education is a progressive discovery of our own ignorance.

Will Durant, American author, 1885-1981
杜朗特,美国作家

Every day I get up and look through the
Forbes list of the richest people in America.
If I'm not there, I go to work.

Robert Orben, American humorist, screenwriter
罗伯特·奥尔本,美国幽默家、电影剧本作家

Everywhere I go I'm asked if I think the university
stifles writers. My opinionis that they don't stifle e-
nough of *them* .

Flannery O'Connor, American author, 1925-1964
奥康纳,美国作家

*Forgive your enemies, but never forget their
names* .

John F. Kennedy, American president, 1917-1963
肯尼迪,美国总统

*For centuries, theologians have been explaining the
unknowable in terms of the-not-worth-knowing* .

Henry Louis Mencken, American editor and critic, 1880-1956
门肯,美国编辑,批评家

*F*ew things are harder to put up with than a good example.

Mark Twain, American writer and humorist, 1835-1910
马克·吐温,美国作家、幽默家

Friends may come and go, but enemies accumulate.

Thomas Jones, American sculptor, 1892-1969
托马斯·琼斯,美国雕塑家

First they ignore you, then they laugh at you, then they fight you, then you win.

*Mahatma Gandhi, Hindu nationalist and spiritual leader,
1869-1948*
甘地,印度民族解放运动领袖

Fill the unforgiving minute with sixty seconds worth of distance run.

Rudyard Kipling, British author, 1865-1936
吉卜林,英国作家

Good teaching is one-fourth preparation and three-fourths theater.

Gail Godwin
戈德温

Grasp the subject, the *words* will follow.

Cato the Elder, 234 -149 B.C.
加图(大)

Give me a museum and I'll fill it.

Pablo Picasso; Spanish painter, 1881-1973
毕加索,西班牙画家

God gave men both a penis and a brain,
but unfortunately not enough blood supply
to run both at the same time.

Robin Williams, commenting on the Clinton Lewinsky affair
威廉斯

He has all the virtues I dislike and none of the
vices I admire.

Sir Winston Churchill, British Prime Minister, 1874-1965
丘吉尔,英国首相

Hell is paved with good Samaritans.

William M. Holden
霍尔顿

He only employs his passion who can make no use of his reason.

Cicero, Roman statesmen, orator and philosopher, 106-43.B.C.

西塞罗,罗马政治家、演说家、哲学家

He who hesitates is a damned fool.

Mae West, American actress, 1892-1980

韦斯特,美国女演员

How wrong it is for a woman to expect the man to build the world she wants, rather than to create it herself.

Anais Nin, American author, 1903-1977

尼恩,美国作家

Hell is other *people*.

Jean-Paul Sartre, French philosopher, 1905-1980

萨特,法国、哲学家

I criticize by creation — not by finding fault.

Cicero, Roman statesmen, orator and philosopher, 106-43 B.C.

西塞罗,罗马政治家、演说家、哲学家

I've just learned about his illness. Let's hope it's nothing trivial.

Irvin S. Cobb, American humorist and author, 1876-1944
科布,美国幽默家、作家

If women didn't exist, all the money in the world would have no meaning.

Aristotle Onassis, Greed shipping magnate, 1906-1975
翁纳西斯,希腊海运大王

If I were two-faced, would I be wearing this one?

Abraham Lincoln, American president, 1809-1865
林肯,美国总统

It is time I stepped aside for a less experienced and less able man.

Anonymous
佚名

I am not young enough to know everything.

Oscar Wilde, Irish writer, playwright, 1854-1900
王尔德,爱尔兰作家、剧作家

If you hear a voice within you say 'you cannot paint,' then by all means paint, and that voice will be silenced.

Vincent Van Gogh, Dutch post-impressionist painter, 1853-1890
凡高,荷兰画家

If knowledge can create problems, it is not through ignorance that we can solve them.

Isaac Asimov, American author, 1920-1992
阿西莫夫,美国作家

I've had a wonderful time, but this wasn't it.

Groucho Marx American comedian, 1895-1977
格劳索·马克斯,美国喜剧演员

It's kind of fun to do the impossible.

Walt Disney, American cartoonist, film producer, 1901-1966
迪斯尼,美国漫画家,电影摄制者

In this life he laughs longest who laughs last.

John Masefield, British author, 1878-1967
梅斯菲尔德,英国作家

In theory, there is no difference between theory and practice. But, in practice, there is.

Jan L. A. van de Snepscheut
斯纳普朔特

I shall not waste my days in trying to prolong them.

Ian L. Fleming, British author, 1908-1964
弗莱明,英国作家

If you can count your money, you don't have a billion dollars.

J. Paul Getty, American oilman, 1892-1976
盖蒂,美国石油商

I find that the harder I work, the more luck I seem to have.

Thomas Jefferson, American author, diplomat, 1743-1826
杰弗逊,美国作家、外交家

In the End, we will remember not the words of our enemies, but the silence of our friends.

Martin Luther King Jr. American clergyman and civil-rights leader, 1929-1968

马丁·路德·金，美国牧师、人权领袖

I can write better than anybody who can write faster, and I can write faster than anybody who can write better.

A. J. Liebling, 1904-1963

利布林

I have often regretted my speech, never my silence.

Xenocrates, Greek philosopher, 396-314 B.C.

色诺克拉底，希腊哲学家

It is much more comfortable to be mad and know it, than to be sane and have one's doubts.

G. B. Burgin

伯金

If you can't sleep, then get up and do something instead of lying there worrying. It's the worry that gets you, not the lack of sleep.

Dale Carnegie, American writer and speaker, 1888-1955

戴尔·卡耐基，美国作家、演说家

I've developed a new philosophy... I only dread one day at a time.

Charlie Brown
布朗

If you want to test your memory, try to recall what you were worrying about one year ago today.

E. Joseph Cossman
科斯曼

I keep the telephone of *my* mind open to peace, harmony, health, love and abundance. Then, whenever doubt, anxiety or fear tries to call me, they keep getting a busy signal — and soon they'll forget my number.

Edith Armstrong
阿姆斯特朗

It is dangerous to be sincere unless **you** are also stupid.

George Bernard Shaw, British playwright and critic, 1856-1950
萧伯纳,英国剧作家、批评家

If you haven't got anything nice to say about anybody, come sit next to me.

Alice Roosevent Longworth
朗沃斯

I heard someone tried the monkeys-on-typewriters bit trying for the plays of W. Shakespeare, but all they got was the collected works of Francis Bacon.

Bill Hirst
赫斯特

I don't know anything about *music*. In my line you don't have to.

Elvis Presley, American entertainer, 1935-1977
普莱斯利,美国演员

I love Mickey Mouse more than any woman I have ever known.

Walt Disney, American cartoonist, film producer, 1901-1966
迪斯尼,美国漫画家、电影摄制者

It was the experience of mystery — even if mixed
with fear — that engendered religion.

Albert Einstein, American theoretical physicist, philosopher, 1875-1955

爱因斯坦,美国理论物理学家、哲学家

In America, anybody can be president. That's one of the
risks you take.

Adlai Stevenson, American statesman, 1900-1965

史蒂文森,美国政治家

I *think* there is a world market for maybe five
computers.

Thomas Watson, Chairman of IBM, 1874-1956

沃森,美国 IBM 总裁

If stupidity got us into this mess, then why
can't it get us out?

Will Rogers, American author and actor, 1879-1935

罗杰斯,美国作家、演员

I have never let my schooling interfere with my education.

Mark Twain, American writer and humorist, 1835-1910

马克·吐温,美国作家、幽默家

It is now possible for a flight atten-
dant to get a pilot pregnant.

Richard J. Ferris, president of United Airlines
里查德·费里斯,美国联合航空公司总裁

It is better to be quotable than to be honest.

Tom Stoppard
斯托帕德

If I had my life to live over, I would perhaps have more actual troubles but I'd
have fewer imaginary ones.

Don Herold
褐罗尔德

If you were plowing a field, which would you
rather use? Two strong oxen or 1024 chickens?

Seymour Cray, father of supercomputing, American computer specialist,
1925-1996
克雷,美国计算机专家

If things go wrong, don't go with them.

Roger Babson, American financial statistician, 1875-1967
巴布森,美国金融统计学家

Imitation is the sincerest form *of* television.

Fred Allen, American hujorist, 1894-1956
艾伦,美国幽默家

In science one tries to tell people, in such a way
as to be understood by everyone, something that
no one ever knew before. But in poetry, it's the
exact opposite.

Paul Dirac, British mathematician and physicist, 1902-1984
迪喇克,英国数学家,物理学家

In any contest between power and patience, bet on patience.

W.B. Prescott
普雷斯克特

*It has become appallingly obvious that our technology
has exceeded our humanity.*

Albert Einstein, American theoretical physicist, philosopher, 1875-1955
爱因斯坦,美国理论物理学家、哲学家

If everything seems under control, you're just not going fast enough.

Mario Andretti
安德烈蒂

I'll sleep when I'm dead.

Warren Zevon, 1947-2003
泽冯

In any moment of decision the best thing you can do is the right thing, the next best thing is the wrong thing, and the worst thing you can do is nothing.

Theodore Roosevelt, 26th President of the United States, 1858-1919
罗斯福,美国第 26 任总统

I don't think necessity is the mother of invention - invention, in my opinion, arises directly from idleness, possibly also from laziness. To save oneself trouble.

Agatha Christie, British author, 1890-1976
克里斯蒂,英国作家

If *you* cannot be a poet, be the poem.

David Carradine, American actor, director
卡拉丹,美国演员、导演

Keep away from people who try to belittle your ambitions. Small people always do that, but the really great make you feel that you, too, can become great.

Mark Twain, American writer and humorist, 1835-1910
马克·吐温,美国作家、幽默家

Knowledge speaks, but wisdom listens.

Jimi Hendrix
亨德里克斯

Let us be of good cheer, remembering that the misfortunes hasdest to bear are those, which will never happen.

James Russel Lowell, American editor, poet and diplomat, 1819-1891
洛厄尔,美国编辑、诗人、外交家

Laugh at yourself first, before anyone else can.

Elsa Maxwell, American columnist, 1883-1963
马克斯韦尔,美国专栏作家

Life is pleasant. Death is peaceful. It's the transition that's troublesome.

Isaac Asimov, American author, 1920-1992

阿西莫夫,美国作家

Love is friendship set on fire.

Jeremy Taylor, British bishop and theologian, 1613-1667

泰勒,英国主教、神学家

Many a man's reputation would not know his character if they met on the street.

Elbert Hubbard, American writer, 1856-1915

埃尔伯特·哈伯德,美国作家

My advice to you is *get married* : if you find a good wife you'll be happy; if not, you'll become a philosopher.

Socrates, Greek philosopher, 470-399 B.C.

苏格拉底,希腊哲学家

Men are not disturbed by things, but the view they take of things.

Epictetus, Greek philosopher, 55-135 A.D.
爱庇克泰德,希腊哲学家

Men and nations behave wisely once they have exhausted all the other alternatives.

Abba Eban, Israeli political leader, 1915-2002
埃班,以色列政治领导人

Men have become the tools of their tools.

Henry David Thoreau, American essayist and poet, 1817-1862
梭罗,美国散文家、诗人

Make everything as simple as possible, *but* not simpler.

Albert Einstein, American theoretical physicist, philosopher, 1875-1955
爱因斯坦,美国理论物理学家、哲学家

Nerves and butterflies are fine — they're physical signs that you're mentally ready and eager. You have to get the butterflies to fly in formation, that's the trick.

Steve Bull
布尔

Nerves provide me with energy. They work for me. It's when I don't have them, when I feel at ease, that I get worried.

Mike Nichols, American comedian, 1931-
尼克尔斯,美国喜剧演员

No one can earn a million dollars honestly.

William Jennings Bryan, American lawyer, 1860-1925
布赖恩,美国律师

No sane man *will dance.*

Cicero, Roman statesmen, orator, philosopher, 106-43 B.C.
西塞罗,罗马政治家、演说家、哲学家

Never interrupt your enemy when he is making a mistake.

Napoleon Bonaparte, French emperor, 1769-1821
拿破仑一世，法国皇帝

Nothing great in the world has been accomplished without passion.

Georg Wilhelm
乔治·威廉

Nothing should be prized more highly than the value of each day.

Johann Wolfgang von Goethe, German writer, scientist, 1749-1832
歌德，德国作家、科学家

Not everything that can be counted counts, and not everything that counts can be counted.

Albert Einstein, American theoretical physicist, philosopher, 1875-1955
爱因斯坦，美国理论物理学家、哲学家

Now, now my good man, this is no time for making enemies.

Voltaire, French philosopher, 1604-1778
伏尔泰，法国哲学家

Never mistake motion for action.

Ernest Hemingway, American writer, 1899-1961

海明威,美国作家

One of the symptoms of an approaching nervous break-down is the belief that one's work is terribly important.

Bertrand Russell, British philosopher, 1872-1970

罗素,英国哲学家

Only two things are infinite, the universe and human stupidity, and I'm not sure about the former.

Albert Einstein, American theoretical physicist, philosopher, 1875-1955

爱因斯坦,美国理论物理学家、哲学家

Once is happenstance. Twice is coincidence. Three times is enemy action.

Auric Goldfinger, 1908-1964

戈德芬德

Only those who will risk going too far can possibly find out how far one can go.

T. S. Eliot, British poet and author

艾略特,英国诗人、作家

Opportunities multiply as they are seized.

Sun Tzu, Chinese military strategist
孙子, 中国兵家

Obstacles are those frightful things you see when you take your eyes off your goal.

Henry Ford, American automobile manufacturer, 1863-1947
亨利·福特, 美国汽车生产商

People everywhere confuse what they read in newspapers with news.

A. J. Liebling, 1904-1963
利布林

People become attached to their burdens sometimes more than the burdens are attached to them.

George Bernard Shaw, British playwright and critic, 1856-1950
萧伯纳, 英国剧作家、批评家

Panic is a sudden desertion of us, and a going over to the enemy of our imagination.

Christian Nevell Bovee
伯维

Perfection is achieved, not when there is nothing more to add, but when there is nothing left to take away.

Antoine de Saint Exupery
艾克萨珀里

People demand freedom of speech to make up for the freedom of thought which they avoid.

Soren Aabye Kierkegaard, Danish philosophy and theologian, 1813-1855
克尔恺郭尔,丹麦哲学家、神学家

People gather bundles of sticks to build bridges they never cross.

Anonymous
佚名

Research is what I'm doing when I don't know what I'm doing.

Wernher Von Braun, American rocket engineer, 1912-1977
布劳恩,美国火箭专家

Sometimes it is not enough to do our best; we must do what is required.

Sir Winston Churchill, British Prime Minister, 1874-1965
丘吉尔,英国首相

Somehow our devils are never quite what we expect when we meet them face to face.

Nelson DeMille
德米尔

Some men see things as they are and ask why. Others dream things that never were and ask why not.

George Bernard Shaw, British playwright and critic, 1856-1950
萧伯纳,英国剧作家、批评家

Sanity is a madness put to *good* uses.

George Santayana, 1863-1952
桑塔纳亚

Some editors are failed writers, **but** so are most writers.

T. S. Eliot, 1888-1965
艾利斯

Success usually comes to those who are **too** busy to be looking for it.

Henry David Thoreau, American essayist and poet, 1817-1862
梭罗,美国散文家、诗人

Sometimes a scream is better than a thesis.

Ralph Waldo Emerson, American author, 1803-1882
爱默生,美国作家

Seek the wisdom of the ages, but look at the world through the eyes of a child.

Ron Wild
罗恩·怀尔德

Some things have to be believed to be seen.

Ralph Hodgson, English poet, 1871-1962
霍奇森,英国诗人

The only thing we have to fear is fear itself.

Franklin d. Roosevelt, American president, 1882-1945
罗斯福,美国总统

There is no such thing in anyone's life as an u-
nimportant day.

Alexander Woollcott, American critic and journalist, 1887-1943

伍尔科特,美国批评家、记者

Talent does what it can; genius does what it must.

Edward George Bulwer-Lytton, 1803-1873

利顿

There are only two ways to live your life.
One is as though nothing is a miracle.
The other is as if everything is.

Albert Einstein, American theoretical physicist, philosopher, 1875-1955

爱因斯坦,美国理论物理学家、哲学家

To be nobody-but-yourself in a world which is doing its best night and day, to make you everybody else
— means to fight the hardest battle which any human
being can fight; and never stop fighting.

E. E. Cummings, American poet, 1894-1962

卡明斯,美国诗人

Time is too slow for those who wait, too swift for those who fear, too long for those who grieve, too short for those who rejoice, but for those who love, time is eternity.

Henry Van Dyke, American author and clergyman
戴克,美国作家、牧师

The future belongs to those who believe in the beauty of their dreams.

Eleanor Roosevelt, American diplomat, author, 1884 - 1962
埃莉诺·罗斯福,美国外交家、作家

The men who try to do something and fail are infinitely better than those who try to do nothing and succeed.

Lloyd Jones
劳艾德·琼斯

There'll be two dates on *your* tombstone. And all your friends will read 'em. But all that's gonna matter is that little dash between 'em...

Kevin Welch
凯文·韦尔奇

Try not to become a man of success. Rather become **a man** of value.

Albert Einstein, American theoretical physicist, philosopher, 1875-1955
爱因斯坦,美国理论物理学家、哲学家

The best way to predict your future is to create it.

Anonymous
佚名

To be **conscious** that you are ignorant is a great step to knowledge.

Benjamin Disrael, British prime minister, diplomat, author, 1804-1881
迪斯累里,英国首相、外交家、作家

Think like a wise man but communicate in the language of the *people*.

William Butler Yeats, Irish writer, 1865-1939
叶芝,爱尔兰作家

The beginning of knowledge is the discovery of something we do not understand.

Frank Herbert, 1920-1986
弗兰克·赫伯特

The **only** way to get rid of a temptation is to yield to it.

Oscar Wilde, Irish writer, playwright, 1854-1900
王尔德,爱尔兰作家、剧作家

The artist is nothing without the gift, but the gift is nothing without

work .

Emile Zola, French author, 1840-1902
左拉,法国作家

The optimist proclaims that we live in the best of all possible worlds, and the pessimist fears this is true.

James Branch Cabell, American author, 1879-1958
卡贝尔,美国作家

The true measure of a man is how he treats someone who can do him absolutely no good.

Samuel Johnson, British author and lexicographer, 1709-1784
塞缪尔·约翰逊,英国作家,词典编纂家

The significant problems we face cannot be solved at the same level of thinking we were at when we created them.

Albert Einstein, American theoretical physicist, philosopher, 1875-1955
爱因斯坦,美国理论物理学家、哲学家

To love oneself is the beginning of a lifelong romance

Oscar Wilde, Irish writer, playwright, 1854-1900
王尔德,爱尔兰作家、剧作家

The nice *thing* about being a celebrity is that if you bore people they think it's their fault.

Henry Kissinger, American scholar, diplomat, 1923-
基辛格,美国学者、外交家

The secret of success is to know something
nobody else knows.

Aristotle Onassis, Greek financier and shipping magnate, 1906-1975
翁纳西斯,希腊金融家、航运巨头

The opposite of a correct statement is a false statement. The opposite of a profound truth may well be
another profound truth.

Niels Henrik David Bohr, Danish physicist, chemist, 1885-1962
玻尔,丹麦物理学家、化学家

There are two ways of constructing a software design;
one way is to make it so simple that there are obviously
no deficiencies, and the other way is to make it so
complicated that there are no obvious deficiencies. The

first method is far *more difficult*.

C. A. R. Hoare
霍尔

Three o'clock is always too late or too
early for anything you want to do.

Jean-Paul Sartre, French author and philosopher, 1905-1980
萨特,法国作家、哲学家

Thank you for sending me a copy of your book —
I'll waste no time reading it.

oses Hadas, 1900-1966
哈达斯

Too many pieces of *music* finish too long after the
end.

Igor Stravinsky, 1882-1971
斯特莱文斯基

The object of war is not to die for your country but
to make the other bastard die for his.

George Patton, American general, 1885-1945
巴顿，美国将军

To sit alone with my conscience will be judg-
ment enough for me.

Charles William Stubbs, British historian, 1825-1901
斯塔布斯，美国历史学家

The best way to predict the future is to invent it.

Alan Kay
艾伦·凯

The longer I live the more I see that I am never wrong about anything, and that all the pains that I have so humbly taken to verify my notions have only wasted **my time.**

George Bernard Shaw, British playwright and critic, 1856-1950

萧伯纳,英国剧作家、批评家

The man who goes alone can start today; but he who travels with another must wait till that other is ready.

Henry David Thoreau, American essayist and poet, 1817-1862

梭罗,美国散文家、诗人

The backbone of surprise is fusing speed with secrecy.

Von Clausewitz, Prussian army officer and military theorist, 1780-1831

克劳斯威茨普鲁士军官,军事理论家

There is only one nature — the division into science and engineering is a human imposition, not a natural one. Indeed, the division is a human failure; it reflects our limited capacity to comprehend the whole.

Bill Wulf

乌尔夫

There's many a bestseller that could have been prevented by a good teacher.

Flannery O'Connor, 1925-1964
奥康纳

This isn't right, this isn't even *wrong*.

Wolfgang Pauli, upon reading a young physicist's paper,
American physicist 1900-1958
波利,美国物理学家

The man who does not read good books has no advantage over the man who cannot read them.

Mark Twain, American writer and humorist, 1835-1910
马克·吐温,美国作家、幽默家

The truth is more important than the facts.

Frank Lloyd Wright, American architect, 1868-1959
莱特,美国建筑家

There are only two tragedies in life: one is not getting
what one wants, and the other is getting it.

Oscar Wilde, Irish writer, playwright, 1854-1900
王尔德,爱尔兰作家、剧作家

There are only two ways to live your
life. One is as though nothing is a
miracle. The other is as though everything is a miracle.

Albert Einstein, American theoretical physicist, philosopher, 1875-1955
爱因斯坦,美国理论物理学家、哲学家

Take a chance! All life is a chance. The person who goes
farthest is generally the one who is willing to do and dare.
The "sure thing" boat never gets far from shore.

Dale Carnegie, American writer and speaker, 1888-1955
戴尔·卡耐基,美国作家、演说家

The essence of greatness is the ability to choose
personal fulfillment in the circumstances where others choose madness.

Dr. Wayne W. Dyer
戴尔

Troubles are a lot like people — they grow bigger if you nurse them.

Anonymous
佚名

The leap into new places is never made in comfort.

Marvin Weisbord
威斯伯尔德

The greatest mistake *you can* make in life is to be continually fearing you will make one.

Elbert Hubbard, American writer, 1856-1915
埃尔伯特·哈伯德,美国作家

We are **more than** what we do... much more than what we accomplish... far more than what we possess.

William Arthur Ward
沃德

When you know a thing, to hold that you know it; and when you do not know a thing, to allow that you do not know it — this is knowledge.

Confucius, Chinese philosopher and educator
孔子,中国哲学家、教育家

We have **too many** high sounding words, and too few actions that correspond with them.

Abigail Adams, American letter writer, 1744-1818
亚当斯,美国书信家

We all agree that your theory is crazy, but is it crazy enough?

Niels Henrik David Bohr , Danish physicist, chemist, 1885-1962
玻尔,丹麦物理学家、化学家

When I am working on a problem I never think about beauty. I only think about how to solve the problem. But when I have finished, if the solution is not beautiful, I know it is wrong.

Buckminster Fuller, American inventor, 1895-1983
富勒,美国发明家

Well-timed silence hath more eloquence than speech.

Martin Farquhar Tupper
塔珀

When choosing between two evils, I always like to try the one I've never tried before.

Mae West, American actress, 1892-1980
韦斯特,美国女演员

Why don't you write books people can read?

wife of Irish author James Joyce, 1882-1941
诺拉·乔伊斯,《尤里西斯》作者乔伊斯之妻

What do you take me for, an idiot?

General Charles de Gaulle, French president, 1890-1970
戴高乐,法国总统

Whether you think that you can, or that you can't, **you are usually right.**

Henry Ford, American automobile manufacturer, 1863-1947
亨利·福特,美国汽车生产商

While we are postponing, life speeds by.

Lucius Annaeus Seneca, Roman philosopher, 4-65. B.C.
塞尼卡,罗马哲学家

Wise *men* make proverbs, but fools repeat them.

Samuel Palmer, 1805-80
帕尔默

We have art to save ourselves from the truth.

Friedrich Nietzsche, German philosopher, 1844-1900
尼采,德国哲学家

We didn't lose the game; we just ran out of **time.**

Vince Lombardi, American football coach, 1913-1970
隆巴迪,美国橄榄球教练

Worrying is like a rocking chair, it gives you something to do, but it gets you nowhere.

Glenn Turner
特纳

What you possess in the world will be found at the day of your death to belong to someone else. But what you are will be yours forever.

Henry Van Dyke, American author and clergyman
戴克,美国作家、牧师

Wagner's music is better than it sounds.

Mark Twain, American writer and humorist, 1835-1910
马克·吐温,美国作家、幽默家

We are not retreating — we are advancing in another *Direction*.

General Douglas MacArthur, American general, 1880-1964
麦克阿瑟,美国将军

Woman was God's second mistake.

Friedrich Nietzsche, German philosopher, 1844-1900
尼采,德国哲学家

Well done is better than well said.

Benjamin Franklin, American statesman, diplomat, 1706-1790

富兰克林,美国政治家、外交家*

Worry never robs tomorrow of its sorrow, it only saps today of its joy.

Leo Buscaglia

巴斯卡格利亚*

You can't wring your hands and roll up your sleeves at the same time.

Pat Schroeder

施罗德*

You got to be careful if you *don't know* where you're going, because you might not get there.

Yogi Berra

贝拉*

148*

You must be the change you wish to see in the world.

Mahatma Gandhi, Hindu nationalist and spiritual leader, 1869-1948
甘地,印度民族解放运动领袖

You can't do anything about the length of your life, but you can do something about its width and depth.

Shira Tehrani
特拉尼

Your choices today determine your tomorrow and you make your life through the power of choice.

Kathy Smith
史密斯

You can only find truth with logic if you have already found truth without it.

Gilbert Keith Chesterton, British author, 1874-1936
切斯特顿,英国作家

You **must** do the thing you think you cannot do.

Eleanor Roosevelt, American diplomat, author, 1884-1962
埃莉诺·罗斯福,美国外交家、作家

Love

爱情

All mankind love a lover.

Ralph Waldo Emerson, American author, 1803-1882
爱默生,美国作家

A kiss: To a young girl, faith; to a married woman, hope; to an old maid, charity.

V. P. Skipper
斯基珀

Absence – that common cure of love.

Miguel de Cervantes, Spanish writer, 1547-1616
塞万提斯,西班牙作家

A beauty is a woman you notice; **A** charmer is one who notices you.

Adlai Stevenson, 1900-1965
史蒂文森

All the little things that make me weak, your eyes and the way you speak without you baby I'm not me...

Britney Spears, American singer, 1981
布兰妮·斯皮尔斯,美国歌手

Always there to dry my tears and make me laugh, that's why I call you my other half.

N. Anonymous
佚名

A compliment is like a kiss through a veil.

Victor Hugo, French poet, dramatist and novelist, 1802-1885
雨果，法国诗人、剧作家、小说家

A friend is one who knows us, but loves us anyway.

Fr. Jerome Cummings
卡明斯

A kiss makes the heart young again and wipes out the years.

Rupert Brooke, American poet, 1887-1915
布鲁克，美国诗人

A kiss is a lovely trick designed by nature to stop speech when words become superfluous.

Ingrid Bergman, Swedish actress
伯格曼，瑞典女演员

A kiss can be a comma, a question mark or an exclamation point. That's basic spelling that every woman ought to know.

Mistinguett, French singer, 1875-1956
米丝廷盖特,法国歌手

A **lover tries to stand in well with the pet dog of the house.**

Moliere, French playwright, 1622-1673
莫利哀,法国剧作家

Age *does not protect you from love but love to some extent protects you from age.*

Jeanne Moreau, French actor
莫罗,法国演员

A priceless moment is when the person that you have fallen in love with, looks you right in the eyes to tell you that they have fallen in love with you.

Anonymous
佚名

A man in love is incomplete until he is married. Then he's finished.

Zsa Zsa Gabor, American actress
柳柏,美国女演员

AND IF BY chance I should hold her, let me hold her for a time. But if allowed just one possession, I would pick her from the garden to be mine.

Anonymous
佚名

A *sweetheart is a bottle of wine, a wife is a wine bottle.*

Baudelaire, French poet, translator,
波德莱尔,法国诗人、翻译家

A woman has got to love a bad man once or twice in her life to be thankful for a *good* one.

Mae West, American actress, 1892-1980
韦斯特,美国女演员

A woman seldom asks advice before she has bought her wedding clothes.

Joseph Addison, English essayist, poet, statesman, 1672-1719
艾迪生,英国散文家、诗人、政治家

A ge does not protect you from love but love to some extent **protects you from age.**

Jeanne Moreau, French actor
莫罗,法国演员

A h Mozart! He was happily married—but his wife wasn't.

Victor Borge, American comedian and pianist, 1909-2000
博格,美国喜剧演员、钢琴家

A ll marriages are happy. It's living together after-wards that is difficult.

Anonymous
佚名

All you need is love .

Lennon and McCartney, British singers in the band Beetles
列农和麦卡尼,英国甲克虫乐队,歌手

157

A man is not where he lives, but where he loves.

Latin proverb
拉丁谚语

A baby is born with a need to be loved-and never outgrows it.

Frank A. Clark, Representative from Florida, 1860-1936
克拉克,美国国会议员

Accept the things to which fate binds you, and love the people with whom fate brings you together, but do so with all your heart.

Marcus Aurelius, Roman freethinker, 1600-1681
奥雷乌斯,罗马自由思想家

*A*s soon go kindle fire with snow, as seek to quench the fire of love with words.

William Shakespeare, English playwright and poet, 1564-1616
莎士比亚,英国剧作家、诗人

*A*t the touch of love everyone becomes a poet.

Plato, Greek philosopher
柏拉图,希腊哲学家

A day in the heaven is a year on earth. A second of waiting for my love to return is a lifetime of torture.

Anonymous
佚名

*A*n ideal wife is one who remains faithful to you but tries to be just as charming as if she weren't.

Sacha Guitry, French filmmaker, dramatist, actor, 1885-1957
吉里特,法国电影制作人、戏剧家、演员

A name makes no matter to me, as long as I can call you my own.

Anonymous
佚名

*A*nd the most unfair thing is to see me here still waiting, patiently, in love with you.

Anonymous
佚名

*B*eing deeply loved by someone gives you strength; loving someone deeply gives you courage.

Lao Zi, Chinese philosopher
老子,中国哲学家

By my eyes I met you
By my soft hands I touched you
By my lips I kissed you
By my heart I loved you!

Anonymous
佚名

*B*efore marriage, a man will lie awake all night thinking about something you said; after marriage, he'll fall asleep before you finish saying it.

Helen Rowland, American writer, 1876-1950
罗兰，美国作家

*B*achelors know more about women than married men; if they didn't, they'd be married too.

Henry Louis Mencken, American newspaperman, book reviewer, 1880-1956
门肯，美国报业者、书评家

*B*y all means marry. If you get a good wife you will become happy, and if you get a bad one you will become a philosopher.

Socrates, Greek philosopher, 470-399 BC
苏格拉底，希腊哲学家

*B*eware you be not swallowed up in books! An ounce of love is worth a pound of knowledge.

John Wesley, American clergyman
威斯利，美国牧师

*C*hoose a wife by your ear than your eye.

Thomas Fuller, British clergyman & historian, 1608-661
托马斯·富勒，英国牧师、历史学家

*C*ome live in my heart and pay no rent.

Samuel Lover, Irish novelist 1797-1868

洛弗,爱尔兰小说家

*C*ourage is like love; it must have hope for nourishment.

Napoleon Bonaparte, French general, 1769-1821

拿破仑,法国将军

*D*on't say you love me unless you really mean it because I might do something crazy like believe it.

Anonymous

佚名

*D*o all things with love.

Og Mandino, American pilot

曼迪诺,美国、飞行员

*D*oes my behavior in respect of love affect nothing? That is because there is not enough love in me.

Albert Schweitzer, German physician and theologian, 1875-1965

施韦策,德国医生、神学家

$\mathcal{E}$ach time I miss you, a star falls down from the sky. So, if you looked up at the sky and found it dark with no stars, it is all your fault. You made me miss you too much!

Anonymous
佚名

$\mathcal{E}$ighty percent of married men cheat in America. The rest cheat in Europe.

Jackie Mason, American comedian
杰基·梅森,美国当代喜剧家

$\mathcal{E}$veryone says you only fall in love once, but that's not true, because every time I see you, I fall in love all over again.

Anonymous
佚名

$\mathcal{E}$veryone admits that love is wonderful and necessary, yet no one agrees on just what it is.

Diane Ackerman, American poet, writer, social worker
阿克曼,美国诗人、作家、社会工作者

Every minute I spend with you is like being in heaven and looking in an angel's eyes.

Anonymous
佚名

*E*ach day you find another reason to amaze me and each day I fall in love with you all over again.

Anonymous
佚名

*E*very day I think about you. Every day I want to be with you ... just so you would know how much I really love you.

Anonymous
佚名

FALLING in love consists merely in uncorking the imagination and bottling the common sense.

Helen Rowland, 1876-1950
罗兰

*F*orever isn't what I want to spend waiting for you, it's what I want us to spend loving each other.

Anonymous
佚名

*F*alling in love doesn't fall by itself. There is always a desire to take the plunge. Just make sure that love sticks around, to pick you up when you fall.

Anonymous
佚名

*F*riendship often ends in love; but love in friend-ship-never.

Charles Caleb Colton, English writer, cleric, merchant, 1780-1832

查尔斯·科尔顿,英国作家、修士、商人

Falling in love with someone isn't always going to be easy. It is often filled with anger and tears. It is when you want to be together despite it all. That

is when you are truly in *Love*.

Anonymous

佚名

*F*or you see, each day I love you more than yes-terday and less than tomorrow.

Rosemonde Gerard, French writer, 1866-1953

杰拉德,法国作家

Gravity *cannot be held responsible for people falling in love.*

Albert Einstein, American theoretical physicist, philosopher, 1875-1955

爱因斯坦,美国理论物理学家、哲学家

Going back with you may be hard, but going forward without you is impossible. I love you.

Anonymous
佚名

Hε that falls in love with himself will have no rivals.

Benjamin Franklin, American statesman, diplomat, 1706-1790
富兰克林,美国政治家、外交家

His kiss is unbelievable, his touch is unforgettable, but my love for him is undeniable!

Anonymous
佚名

Hate leaves ugly scars, love leaves beautiful ones.

Mignon McLaughlin
麦克劳林

He to whom this emotion is a stranger, who can no longer pause to wonder and stand rapt in awe, is as good as dead: his eyes are closed.

Albert Einstein, American theoretical physicist, philosopher, 1875-1955
爱因斯坦,美国理论物理学家、哲学家

"*How* long have we been together?" is the question. "Not long enough" is the answer.

Anonymous
佚名

Hatred paralyzes life; **love releases it**.
Hatred confuses life; **love harmonizes it**.
Hatred darkens life; **love illumines it**.

*Martin Luther King, Jr., African-American civil
rights leader, 1929-1968*
马丁·路德·金，美国黑人人权领袖

I could say that you complete me...but that would be a lie, because every morning when I wake I long for you more than the day before.

Anonymous
佚名

I *may not be the dream you want to come true, but I'll always be the person in love with you.*

Anonymous
佚名

In the arithmetic of love, one plus one equals everything, and two minus one equals nothing.

Mignon McLaughlin
麦克劳林

Look into my heart and see what I am saying, for my heart speaks the truth and the truth is I love you.

Anonymous
佚名

If you *live to be a hundred, I want to live to be ninety-nine so I never have to live without you.*

Anonymous
佚名

It's your love... it just does something to me. It sends a shock right through me... I can't get enough.

Tim McGraw
麦格劳

I'm afraid to admit that I'm in love with you, but I can't forget your eyes and I can't stop feeling your lips; your words keep echoing in my head and you always make me weak. I don't want to mean it when I say, "I love you", but I can't help it.

Anonymous
佚名

I wrote your name in the sand, but the waves washed it away. I wrote your name on a piece of paper, but it got thrown away. I wrote your name in the sky, but the wind blew it away. So, I wrote your name in my heart and that's where it will stay.

Anonymous
佚名

It's better to have loved and lost than to do forty pounds of laundry a week.

Laurence J Peter, American educator and writer, 1919-98
彼得，美国教育家、作家

*I*f you were a tear in my eye, I would not cry for fear of losing you.

Anonymous
佚名

I but know that I love thee, whatever thou art.

Thomas Moore, Irish poet, 1779-1852
穆尔，苏格兰诗人

I remember the last time I saw that sparkle in your eye — when I realized there was a beautiful angel by my side.

Anonymous
佚名

I would be lying if I said you stepped out of my dreams and into my life... My dreams were never this wonderful!

Anonymous
佚名

It is better to have loved and lost Than never to have loved at all .

Alfred Lord Tennyson, 1809-1892
丁尼生

I can forgive you for everything , except for not understanding that I was in love with you .

Anonymous
佚名

I do not know how much I love you , but I do know how much more I wish to .

Anonymous
佚名

It is astonishing how little one feels alone when one loves.

John Bulwer, *British linguist*, 1606-1656
布尔沃,英国语言学家

If I had the whole world to write on to express how much I love you , it wouldn't all fit.

Anonymous
佚名

I want to stare into your eyes and never look away; I want you to hold me in your arms and tell me it's okay; I want to kiss with a passion that only we can share, and when it all falls down I want you to be there.

Anonymous
佚名

I've been in love with the same woman for forty-one years. If my wife finds out, she'll kill me.

Henry Youngman, American comedian, 1906-1998
亨利·扬曼，美国喜剧演员

*O*n you I find the completion of me and the wonder of us.

Anonymous
佚名

If **I love you, what business is it of yours?**

Johann Wolfgang von Goethe, German writer,
1749-1832
歌德，德国作家

I *need many things to help me live, but I need only you to make life worth living.*

Anonymous
佚名

*I*t seems like nothing had happened until I had shared them with you.

Chris Carrabba
卡拉巴

170

I never thought love could be so magnificent until I saw the sincere look in your eyes, telling me that this time...I would never shed another tear.

Anonymous
佚名

I love you, **these three words could change our lives forever, but for you, I will take that chance.**

Anonymous
佚名

If you ask me why I've changed, all I gotta do is say your sweet name.

Tim McGraw
格劳

I asked for light, God gave me the sun, I asked for water, God gave me rain, I asked for happiness, and God gave me you.

Anonymous
佚名

I love you not only for who you are, but *for who I am when I am with you!*

Anonymous
佚名

In love the paradox occurs that two beings become one and yet remain two.

Erich Fromm, German psychoanalyst and social theorist, 1900-1980

艾里克·弗罗姆,德国心理分析家、社会理论家

It's not being in love that makes me happy. It's being in love with you that makes me **happy**.

Anonymous

佚名

If you judge people, you have no time to love them.

Mother Theresa, Indian nun, Nobel Peace Prize Winner, 1910-1997

特里萨,印度修女、诺贝尔和平奖获得者

I know I'm in love because around you my heart beats both faster and slower at the same time.

Anonymous

佚名

If you told me you loved me, I could deal with that. If you told me you were walking away, I could deal with that. But, I cannot deal if you tell me you love me but you are walking away.

Anonymous

佚名

IMMATURE love says："I love you because I need you." Mature love says："I need you because I love you."

Erich Fromm, German psychoanalyst, 1900-1980
艾里克·弗罗姆,德国心理分析家、社会理论家

In love,
If you risk nothing,
You risk everything!

Anonymous
佚名

If *I could choose one day to live over again, it would be the day I met you.*

Anonymous
佚名

I don't wish to be everything to everyone, but I would like to be something to someone.

Javan
贾范

I *gaze up at the sun, and I'm comforted because I know that the same sun's light is lighting your face.*

Anonymous
佚名

I love him for the things he has, and despite the things he doesn't have.

Anonymous
佚名

I have found the paradox that if I love until it hurts, then there is no hurt, but only more love.

Mother Theresa, Indian nun, Nobel Peace Prize Winner, 1910-1997
特里萨，印度修女、诺贝尔和平奖获得者

I'D rather spend a lifetime with you than to live all the ages of this world alone.

Anonymous
佚名

I may not be the perfect guy in your life, But I will never be out of your life. It means "Forever".

Anonymous
佚名

It's not my fault I love you, It's yours.

Anonymous
佚名

In true love the smallest distance is too great, and the greatest distance can be bridged.

Hans Nouwens
汉斯·诺文斯

I may have cried a million times since we haven't been together, but all the times you made me smile is what will remain in my heart forever.

Anonymous
佚名

If *you truly love someone, then the only thing you want for them is to be happy.... even if it's not with you*

Lauren
劳伦

If you love someone put their name in a circle, not a heart, because hearts can be broken but circles go on forever!

Anonymous
佚名

I **was in a cathedral when I got down on my knees and worshipped you, mistook you for an angel without those two celestial wings.**

Anonymous
佚名

If you press me to say why I loved him, I can say no more than because he was he, and I was I.

Michel de Montaigne, French essayist, 1533-1592
蒙田,法国散文家

If loving you makes a slave of me, then I'll spend my whole life in chains.

Anonymous
佚名

If you ask me how I knew that I love you, I'll tell you that I just knew.

Anonymous
佚名

I may not get to see you as often as I like. I may not get to hold you in my arms all through the night. But deep in my heart I truly know, you're the one that I love, and I can't let you go.

Niki
尼奇

If we are just friends, then tell me, why do I feel like we are much more?

Anonymous
佚名

If we transcend the limits of our mind, we can cease merely living and begin to be one together.

Anonymous
佚名

I never thought that I would meet someone who was so hard to forget.

Anonymous
佚名

I am looking for someone, who can take as much as I give, give back as much as I need, and still have the will to live. I am intense, I am in need, I am in pain, I am in love.

Anonymous
佚名

I'd rather have bad times with you, than good times with someone else.

Luther Vandross
范德罗斯

If loving you is wrong, I never want to be right again.

Anonymous
佚名

In dreams and in love there are no impossibilities.

Janos Arany, Hungarian poet, 1817-1882
阿兰尼,匈牙利诗人

It is better for girl to sleep a hundred years and be kissed and awakened by the right prince than to stay awake and be kissed a hundred times by the wrong frog.

Anonymous
佚名

Of you love something, set it free. If it comes back, it's yours. If it does not come back, it was never meant to be.

Anonymous
佚名

*I*t's not whether you get knocked down. **Its whether you get up again.**

Vince Lombardi
隆巴迪

If this letter doesn't reach its destination, *send it to heaven'cause it was meant for an angel.*

Anonymous
佚名

If she is my best and first choice, then second best must be an angel whose beauty would defy the goddesses themselves.

Anonymous
佚名

If ever you think of me out of the blue, just remember it's all the kisses I've blown in the air finally catching up with you!

Christina
克里斯蒂娜

I love you more than any word can say ... I love you more than every action I take ... I'll be right here loving you till the end.

Anonymous
佚名

I'm totally drunk with joy and happiness when I'm with you!

Anonymous
佚名

If you love somebody, let them go. If they return, they were always yours. If they don't, they never were.

Anonymous
佚名

I have said nothing because there is nothing I can say that would describe how I feel as perfectly as you deserve it.

Kyle Schmidt, German singer
史密德, 德国歌手

I see you when I'm dreaming, even more when I'm awake. You rob from my soul and it is my heart you take.

Anonymous
佚名

If distance were measured in terms of the heart we'd never be more than a minute apart.

Anonymous
佚名

I'd rather die tomorrow than live a hundred years without knowing you.

John Smith
约翰·史密斯

If fate locks the door, go in through the window.

Anonymous
佚名

It's not who you are to the world, it's who you are to me. It's not how many times I say I love you... it's how much I really do.

Anonymous
佚名

I would rather live and love where death is king than have eternal life where love is not.

Robert Green Ingersoll
英格索尔

It rains because the heavens miss the star that has fallen to earth. That star is you.

Anonymous
佚名

I hate him for leaving when I thought he never would ... but I love him for staying when I was putting him through so much.

Anonymous
佚名

Just as the sunbeam cannot separate itself from the sun and the wave cannot separate itself from the sea, I cannot separate myself from you. You are a part of me and I, a part of you.

Anonymous
佚名

Just because someone doesn't love you the way you want them to doesn't mean they don't love you with all they have.

Anonymous
佚名

Life is the flower for which love is the honey.

Victor Hugo, French poet, dramatist and novelist,
1802-1885
雨果，法国诗人、剧作家、小说家

Life without love is like a tree without blossoms or fruit.

Kahlil Gibran, Lebanon poet, philosopher,
and artist, 1883-1931
纪伯伦，黎巴嫩诗人、哲学家、艺术家

Loving someone doesn't need a reason. If you can explain why you love someone, it's not called "Love"... it's called "Like"

H. Darrel
达雷尔

Love purely and be happy it came in your way. If it hurts you then be glad because you've been touched by Love.

Anonymous
佚名

Love, and a cough, cannot be hid.

George Herbert
赫伯特

*L*ove makes time pass; time makes love pass.

French proverb
法国谚语

*L*ove and work are the cornerstones of our humanness.

Sigmund Freud, Austrian psychiatrist, 1856-1939
弗洛伊德,奥地利心理学家

*L*ove will find its way through paths where wolves would fear to prey.

Anonymous
佚名

*L*ove does not consist in gazing at each other, but in looking outward together in the same direction.

Antoine de Saint Exupery
艾克萨珀里

*L*ove is stronger than justice.

Sting, American singer
斯汀,美国歌手

*L*ove never says, "I have done enough."

Anonymous
佚名

*L*ove means never having to say you're sorry.

Erich Segal, American novelist, dramatist
西格尔,美国小说家、剧作家

Love is when you don't have to be with another person to touch their heart!

Anonymous
佚名

Love is the heart of the soul.

Robert Paul
罗伯特·保尔

Love is like a hole; once you fall in, it's hard to get out.

Anonymous
佚名

Love is a state in which a man sees things most decidedly as they are not.

Friedrich Nietzsche, German philosopher, 1844-1900
尼采,德国哲学家

Love is the heart of the soul.

Robert Paul
罗伯特·保尔

Love is a state in which a man sees things most decidedly as they are not.

Friedrich Nietzsche, German philosopher, 1844-1900
尼采,德国哲学家

Love itself is unstable... it is you and I who keep it balanced.

Anonymous
佚名

Looking back, I have this to regret, that too often when I loved, I did not say so.

David Grayson, 1890-1990
格雷森

Love is the thing that enables a woman to sing while she mops up the floor after her husband has walked across it in his barn boots.

Hoosier Farmer, 1919-1999
法默

Love is an exploding cigar we willingly smoke.

Lynda Barry, cartoonist, novelist
巴里,漫画家、小说家

Love is the Law of our Being.

Mohandas K. Gandhi, Indian spiritual and nationalist
leader, 1869-1948
甘地,印度精神领袖、民族领袖

Love is what we were born with. Fear is what we learned here.

Marianne Williamson, American religious figure and lecturer
威廉姆森,美国宗教人物、演讲者

Love isn't love until you give it away.

Anonymous
佚名

Love is much like a wild rose, beautiful and calm, but willing to draw blood in its defense.

Mark Overby
奥弗比

Love is a sweet tyranny, because the lover endureth his torments willingly.

Proverb
谚语

Love is the triumph of imagination over intelligence.

Henry Louis Mencken, American essayist, 1880-1956
门肯,美国散文家

Love and respect are the most important aspects of parenting, and of all relationships.

Jodie Foster, author
福斯特,作家

*L*ove has given me wings, so I must fly.

Anonymous
佚名

*L*ove is an act of endless forgiveness, a tender look that becomes a habit.

Peter Ustinov, British actor and writer, 1921-2004
乌斯提诺夫,英国演员、作家

Love is the silent saying and saying of a single name.

Mignon McLaughlin
麦克劳林

Love looks not with the eyes, but with the mind, and therefore is winged Cupid painted blind.

William Shakespeare, English playwright and poet, 1564-1616
莎士比亚,英国剧作家、诗人

Love is a game that two can play and both win.

Eva Gabor, Actress, 1939-1969
爱娃,演员

Love is not blind — it sees more, not less. But because it sees more, it is willing to see less.

Rabbi Julins Gordon
戈顿

Love is a gross exaggeration of the difference between one person and everybody else.

George Bernard Shaw, British playwright and critic, 1856-1950
萧伯纳,英国剧作家、批评家

Love is like dew that falls on both nettles and lilies.

Swedish Proverb
瑞典谚语

Love rules its kingdom without a sword.

English Proverb
英国谚语

Love conquers all.

Virgil, Roman poet, 1st century B.C.
维吉尔,罗马诗人

Love understands love; it needs no talk.

Frances Ridley Havergal, English poet, 1836-1879
哈弗格尔,英国诗人

Love is so confusing — you tell a girl she looks great and what's the first thing you do? Turn out the lights!

Robert Orben, American humorist
罗伯特·奥尔本,美国幽默家

*L*ove ceases to be a pleasure, when it ceases to be a secret.

Aphra Behn, British writer, 1640-1689
贝恩,英国作家

Love is, above all, the gift of oneself.

Jean Anouilh, French playwright, 1910-1987
阿诺伊,法国剧作家

Love's way of dealing with us is different from conscience's way. Conscience commands; love inspires.

Arnold Joseph Toynbee, British historian, 1889-1975
汤恩比,英国历史学家

Love is a smoke made with the fume of sighs.

William Shakespeare, English playwright and poet, 1564-1616
莎士比亚,英国剧作家、诗人

Love is my religion — I could die for it.

John Keats, British poet, 1795-1821
济慈,英国诗人

Love never claims, it ever gives.

Mohandas K. Gandhi, Indian nationalist and spiritual leader, 1869-1948
甘地,印度民族领袖、精神领袖

Love is a feeling, a feeling of happiness. Love is powerful, too powerful to play with. This feeling is strange and hard to describe, but when you fall in love, you will know it inside.

Anonymous
佚名

Love cannot be cured by herbs.

Ovid, Roman poet, 43-17 BC
奥维德,罗马诗人

*L*ove is a choice you make from moment to moment.

Barbara De Angelis
安杰利斯

*L*ife has taught us that love does not consist in gazing at each other but in looking outward together in the same direction.

Lewis Galanti è re, American translator
加兰提尔,美国翻译家

Love took me by the hand; love took me by surprise; love led me to you, and love opened up my eyes.

Michelle Branch
布兰奇

Love is not *50/50*, it is not give and take. In love each partner gives *100%* and takes nothing in return.

Anonymous
佚名

Love makes the world go around.

English proverb
英国谚语

*L*ove is the most difficult and dangerous form of courage. CourWge is the most desperate, admirable and noble kind of love.

Delmore Schwartz
舒尔茨

Love cures people, both the ones who give it and the ones who receive it.

Dr. Karl Augustus Menninger, American psychiatrist, 1893-1990
门宁格,美国精神病学家

Love does not begin and end the way we seem to think it does. Love is a battle, love is a war; love is a growing up.

James Baldwin, American writer, 1924-1987
鲍德温,美国作家

Love takes off masks that we fear we cannot live without and know we cannot live within.

James Baldwin, American writer, 1924-1987
鲍德温,美国作家

Love has nothing to do with what you are expecting to get, it's what you are expected to give - which is everything.

Anonymous
佚名

Love builds bridges where there are none.

R. H. Delaney
德拉尼

Love **looks through a telescope; envy, through a microscope.**

Josh Billings, American writer, 1818-1885
比林斯,美国作家

Love is like a violin. The music may stop now and then, but the strings remain forever.

June Masters Bacher
巴彻

Love is the only force capable of transforming an enemy into friend.

Martin Luther King, Jr., African-American civil rights leader, 1929-1968

马丁·路德·金,美国黑人人权领袖

Love is easy to spot, when someone has found it!

Confusious

孔子

*L*ove one another and you will be happy. It's as simple and as difficult as that.

Michael Leunig, Australian cartoonist

勒尼格,澳大利亚漫画家

*L*ove is the great miracle cure. Loving ourselves works miracles in our lives.

Louise Hay, American mathematician, 1935-1989

海,美国数学家

*L*ove is shown in your deeds, not in your words.

Fr. Jerome Cummings

卡明斯

*L*ove is an emotion experienced by the many and enjoyed by the few.

George Jean Nathan, American drama critic, 1882-1958

内森,美国戏剧批评家

My love to you is everlasting; it will never grow old and it will never fade away. I will forever love you.

Anonymous
佚名

My love no longer depends on the way you treat me.

Rainer Maria Rilke, German writer, 1875-1926
里尔克,德国作家

My love for you is as much a part of the universe as the sun, moon and stars; the only difference is my love will last longer.

Anonymous
佚名

My heart belongs to you. I know because I feel complete when you're around.

Anonymous
佚名

Man wants to be a woman's first love, a woman wants to be his last.

Oscar Wilde, Irish writer, playwright, 1854-1900
王尔德,爱尔兰作家、剧作家

My life began the day I met you.

Anonymous
佚名

M inutes and hours and years may go by, but my heart knows nothing of time. So don't cry, just keep me right there in your dreams, and hold on to these words of mine.

Reba McEntire
麦肯泰尔

M en love because they are afraid of them-selves, afraid of the loneliness that lives in them, and need someone in whom they can lose them-selves as smoke loses itself in the sky.

V. F. Calverton, American literary critic, historian, 1900-1940
卡尔弗顿，美国文学批评家、历史学家

N obody has ever measured, even poets, how much a heart can hold.

Zelda Fitzgerald, American writer, 1900-1948
菲兹杰拉德，美国作家

N obody is perfect until you fall in love with them.

Anonymous
佚名

NOW join your hands, and with your hands your heart.

William Shakespeare, English playwright and poet, 1564-1616

莎士比亚,英国剧作家、诗人

No man is worth your tears, and the one who is will not make you cry.

Anonymous

佚名

Now I know how the river feels, when it reaches the sea and finally finds the place it was always meant to be. Holding fast, home at last, knowing the journey is through. Laying here with you, I know how the river feels.

Nickel Creek

克里克

Never forget to find yourself, for without you there is nothing left for me to love.

Anonymous

佚名

Never frown when you are sad, you never know who is falling in love with your smile.

Anonymous

佚名

No one realizes the beauty of love, until you're caught in it.

Anonymous

佚名

Olivia; *Love sought is good, but given unsought is better.*

William Shakespeare, English playwright and poet, 1564-1616
莎士比亚,英国剧作家、诗人

Our whole relationship is one big inside joke that no one will understand but you and me.

Anonymous
佚名

*O*n the darkest nights and coldest days, catching you with a glimpse of my eye warms my heart and my soul.

Anonymous
佚名

*O*ther people save lives, but you rescued my soul.

Anonymous
佚名

One night, the moon said to me, "If he makes you cry, why don't you leave him?" I looked at the moon and said, "Moon, would you ever leave your sky?"

Anonymous
佚名

Patience with others is Love; Patience with self is Hope; Patience with God is Faith.

Adel Bestavros
贝斯塔夫罗斯

*P*assion makes the world go round. Love just makes it a safer place.

Anonymous
佚名

*P*eople need loving the most when they deserve it the least.

John Harrigan
哈里根

Remember, *you can be in love, but always be independent; be your own person.*

Anonymous
佚名

*S*ometimes the heart sees what is invisible to the eye.

H. Jackson Brown Jr. , American writer
布朗,美国作家

*S*ometimes just holding hands is holding on to everything.

Anonymous
佚名

*S*ome women love only what they can hold in their arms; others, only what they can't.

Mignon McLaughlin
麦克劳林

So dear I love him, that with him all deaths I could endure, without him live no life.

John Milton, British poet, 1608-1674
弥尔顿，英国诗人

Sometimes I wish I had never met you because then I could go to bed at night not knowing there was someone like you out there.

Anonymous
佚名

Someone asked my girl, "Do you know where heaven is?" and she said softly back, "Right between his arms."

Inches
英奇斯

Teach me how to dream for I only know how to dream about you.

Anonymous
佚名

The greatest healing therapy is friendship and love.

Hubert H. Humphrey, 36th American vice president, 1911-1978
汉弗莱，美国副总统

They said angels were supposed to come from the sky, that means I'm lucky, cause one fell for me.

Anonymous
佚名

There is a courtesy of the heart; it is allied to love. From it springs the purest courtesy in the outward behavior.

Johann Wolfgang von Goethe, German writer,
scientist, 1749-1832
歌德,德国作家、科学家

Time passes quickly when you are in love and you can never get enough of the other person.

Anonymous
佚名

To fear love is to fear life, and those who fear life are already three parts dead.

Bertrand Russell, British philosopher, 1872-1970
罗素,英国哲学家

The way to love anything is to realize that it might be lost.

Gilbert Keith Chesterton, British author, 1874-1936
切斯特顿,英国作家

The world is a puzzle and we're two pieces that fit perfectly together.

Anonymous
佚名

Tell me who admires you and loves you, and I will tell you who you are.

Charles Augustin Sainte-Beauve, French poet, critic and historian, 1804-1869
圣伯弗,法国诗人、批评家、历史学家

There are times I want to get mad, there are times I want to give you up, there are times I want to cry but no matter how many times I think of this, I always end up saying: I love you very much!

Anonymous
佚名

True love isn't so much a dreamy feeling that you have as it is an enduring commitment to give sacrificially – even, or perhaps especially, when you don't feel like it.

William R. Mattox, Jr., American writer
马托克斯,美国作家

Time passes quickly when you are in love and you can never get enough of the other person.

Anonymous
佚名

The first duty of love is to listen.

Paul Tillich, theologian and writer, 1886-1965
蒂利希,神学家、作家

To love is to have a heart; to be in love, is to make it beat.

Anonymous
佚名

This is the miracle that happens every time to those who really love; the more they give, the more they possess.

Rainer Maria Rilke, German writer, 1875-1926
里尔克,德国作家

The seed of greatness in a man begins to blossom when the right woman is there to water it.

Anonymous
佚名

The best and most beautiful things in this world cannot be seen or even heard, but must be felt with the heart.

Helen Keller, American author and lecturer, 1880-1968
海伦·凯勒,美国作家、演讲家

The *sparkle in your eyes could make the stars jealous.*

Anonymous
佚名

$\mathcal{T}$here is no fear in love, but perfect love casts our fear.

John, Christian apostle, 1st century
约翰,基督圣徒

$\mathcal{T}$hey say loving you is my biggest mistake but how can it be so wrong if it feels so right? If ever I made a mistake, its not that I love you, its thinking that someday you'll love me too...

Tamz
塔姆兹

$\mathcal{T}$o the world you may only be one person, but to one person you may be the world.

Anonymous
佚名

$\mathcal{T}$o let a fool kiss you is stupid, to let a kiss fool you is worse.

Philippos
菲利波斯

$\mathcal{T}$o be in love is to be living a dream come true.

Anonymous
佚名

*T*ake away love and our earth is a tomb.

Robert Browning, British poet, 1812-1889

布朗宁,英国诗人

There is a star in your eye that only I can see. There is a place in your heart where only I want to be.

Anonymous

佚名

*T*rue love is found where we cannot accept the one we love to be absent in our lives.

Philippos

菲利波斯

*T*hey say nothing in the world is perfect but I know one exception, the joining of our two hearts.

Anonymous

佚名

The hunger for love is much more difficult to remove than the hunger for bread.

Mother Theresa, Indian nun, Nobel Peace Prize Winner, 1910-1997

特里萨,印度修女、诺贝尔奖获得者

The love we give away is the only love we keep.

Elbert Hubbard, American writer, 1856-1915
埃尔伯特·哈伯德，美国作家

To love and to be loved is the greatest joy on earth.

Anonymous
佚名

he course of true love never did run smooth.

William Shakespeare, English playwright and poet, 1564-1616
莎士比亚，英国剧作家、诗人

The beauty of love is to look into your eyes, and see the love you feel for me, to see the way you feel and the way you care, that is why I love you.

Anonymous
佚名

The art of love... is largely the art of persistence.

Albert Ellis, American psychotherapist
埃利斯，美国精神病医生

To be in love is to feel you could touch a star without standing on tiptoe.

Anonymous
佚名

The hardest-learned lesson: that people have only their kind of love to give, not our kind.

Mignon McLaughlin
麦克劳林

There are some things in life that can be said using words, but the true explanations of feelings come from the heart.

Anonymous
佚名

The things that people in love do to each other they remember, and if they stay together it's not because they forget, it's because they forgive.

Anonymous
佚名

The best proof of love is trust.

Joyce Brothers, American psychologist
乔伊斯兄弟，美国心理学家

The greatest beauty on earth is found in the hearts of those who love.

Anonymous
佚名

$\mathscr{T}$he space between your heart and mine is the space we'll fill with time.

Dave Matthews Band
班德

$\mathscr{T}o$ love is to cherish and to cherish to keep it close to your heart.

Anonymous
佚名

$\mathscr{T}o$ be capable of steady friendship or lasting love, are the two greatest proofs, not only of goodness of heart, but of strength of mind.

Paul Aubuchon
奥布乔翁

$\mathscr{T}$he smallest word I know is "I", the sweetest word I know is "love", and the only thing that will remind me of that will be "you".

Anonymous
佚名

$\mathscr{W}$hen love is not madness, it is not love.

Pedro Calderon de la Barca, Spanish playwright, 1600-1681
卡尔德隆，西班牙剧作家

*W*henever you see love coming, welcome it with open arms and let it enter into you. People will ask, "Are you in love?" You will say, "No, love is in me."

Anonymous
佚名

*W*hen one is in love, one always begins by deceiving oneself, and one always ends by deceiving others. That is what the world calls a romance.

Oscar Wilde, Irish writer, playwright, 1854-1900
王尔德,爱尔兰作家、剧作家

*W*ithout love, the rich and poor live in the same house.

Anonymous
佚名

*W*e are all born for love. It is the principle of existence, and its only end.

Benjamin Disraeli, England's prime minister, 1804-1881
本杰明·迪斯雷利,英国首相

*W*hen you would die for that special someone, that's when you know that you are in love.

Anonymous
佚名

*W*hen you smile, I melt inside.

Tara
塔拉

Why do you always leave me speechless? I guess you could answer, but I wouldn't be able to respond.

Jacqui
雅克

*W*hen I saw you I liked you, when I liked you I loved you, when I loved you I lost you.

Anonymous
佚名

*W*e look forward to the time when the power to love will replace the love of power. Then will our world know the blessing of peace.

William Gladstone, British statesman and orator, 1809-1898
格莱斯顿，英国政治家、演说家

*W*hen tomorrow starts without me, don't think we are far apart, for every time you think of me I am right in your heart.

Anonymous
佚名

When you welcome love with your whole heart, soul and body, love will welcome you with all its sweetness.

Akidimah
阿基迪马

Winning your heart is the ultimate gift in the world, and losing your heart is ultimately the worst.

Anonymous
佚名

We cannot really love anybody with whom we never laugh.

Agnes Repplier, American essayist, 1855-1950
雷普利尔,美国散文家

Who, being loved, is poor?

Oscar Wilde, Irish writer, playwright, 1854-1900
王尔德,爱尔兰作家、剧作家

When I close my eyes you're everywhere, but when I am awake you're never there.

Anonymous
佚名

*We can do not great things-only small things
with great love.*

Mother Theresa, Albanian-born Indian nun, Nobel Peace Prize
Winner, 1910-1997
特里萨，印度修女、诺贝尔奖获得者

Whenever I want you, all I have to do...
is dream.

Anonymous
佚名

What *the world really needs is more love and
less paper work.*

Pearl Bailey, American entertainer, 1918-1990
贝利，美国艺人

What's worse, falling in love with a
fool or being a fool for falling in love?

Anonymous
佚名

*When love and skill work together, expect a master-
piece.*

John Ruskin, British art critic, 1819-1900
罗斯金，英国艺术评论家

When I see you, the world stops as if the only purpose in life was for me to please you.

Anonymous
佚名

When I look into his eyes, it seems all the problems in the world go away and I'm floating in mid-air.

Sabine
萨拜因

When life is too crazy, and things are moving too fast, look to the constant stars... and remember, like them, our love can last.

Anonymous
佚名

*W*here there is love there is life.

Mahatma Gandhi, Hindu nationalist and spiritual leader, 1869-1948
甘地,印度民族解放运动领袖

*W*ith love and patience, nothing is impossible.

Daisaku Ikeda
艾迪达

212

When you find love never let it go-it's a long fall down from the clouds.

Anonymous
佚名

When I saw you I fell in love, and you smiled because you knew.

William Shakespeare, English playwright and poet, 1564-1616
莎士比亚,英国剧作家、诗人

When I saw you I was afraid to meet you,
When I met you I was afraid to know you,
When I knew you I was afraid to love you,
Now I love you and I'm afraid to lose you!

Anonymous
佚名

Where love is concerned, too much is not even enough.

Pierre De Beaumarchais, French dramatist, 1732-1799
博马舍,法国剧作家

*W*hen he is the cause of your inspiration, when the world appears under a wonderful new light, when suddenly the meaning of your life is obvious, then you are in love.

Anonymous
佚名

*W*here there is great love, there are always wishes.

Willa Cather, American writer, 1873-1947
卡瑟，美国作家

*W*hen we love, it isn't because the person's perfect, it's because we learn to see an imperfect person perfectly.

Anonymous
佚名

*W*ho would give a law to lovers? Love is unto itself a higher law.

Boethius, Roman philosopher, 524
波伊提乌，罗马哲学家

*W*e loved with a love that was more than love.

Edgar Allan Poe, American poet, 1809-1849
坡，美国诗人

When you love someone all your saved up wishes start coming true.

Anonymous
佚名

Wisdom begins in wonder.

Socrates, Greek philosopher, 470-399 B.C.
苏格拉底,希腊哲学家

We come to love not by finding a perfect person, but by learning to see an imperfect person perfectly.

Sam Keen
基恩

*W*hen in love, sometimes it's worse to win a fight than to lose.

Billie Holiday, American jazz singer, 1915-1959
霍利迪,美国爵士乐歌手

*W*hen you fall in love with someone, you give them your heart. When you find out they love you too, you get it back, times two.

Anonymous
佚名

We choose those we like; with those we love, we have no say in the matter.

Mignon McLaughlin
麦克劳林

*W*hen a man is in love or in debt, someone else has the advantage.

Bill Balance
巴兰斯

When you're soaring through the air, I'll be your solid ground. Take every chance you dare, I'll still be there when you come back down.

Nickle Creek
克里克

*Y*ou don't love a woman because she is beautiful, but she is beautiful because you love her.

Anonymous
佚名

You will find as you look back upon your life that the moments when you have truly lived are the moments when you have done things in the spirit of love.

Henry Drummond, Canadian poet, scientist, 1851-1897
德拉蒙德,加拿大诗人、科学家

You never know how much a person means to you until you lose them; don't take anyone for granted.

Anonymous
佚名

You've got to follow your passion. You've got to figure out what it is you love–who you really are. And have the courage to do that. I believe that the only courage anybody ever needs is the courage to follow your own dreams.

Oprah Winfrey
奥普拉·温弗里

You know you're in love when you don't wanna go to sleep at night because your life is better than a dream.

Anonymous
佚名

You learn to like someone when you find out what makes them laugh, but you can never truly love someone until you find out what makes them cry.

Anonymous
佚名

You know you truly love someone when every day you meet is like the first time you fall in love.

Anonymous
佚名

You know you're in love when at those times you're apart, you find yourself gazing at the sky in the direction she lives and feeling some peace in knowing that you live under the same sky.

Anonymous
佚名

You know that you're in love when you freeze up for the first time in your life — my feet were frozen to the elevator floor, but my heart was screaming to take one step closer and give her a kiss.

Anonymous
佚名

Your eyes, as we said our good-byes, can't get them out of my mind. And I find I can't hide from your eyes, the ones that took me by surprise, the night you came into my life. Where there's moonlight, I see your eyes.

Anonymous
佚名

You haven't found the right person if you can live with them, you've found the right person if you can't live without them.

You are far away, but yet your love remains, I can feel it all around. It embraces me and holds me tight, night after night.

YOU know you're in love when just thinking about the person who gives you butterflies. Then years later, the butterflies are just as strong.

You know you're in love when you can still feel his kiss on your lips after he's gone.

You don't have to love in words, because even through the silences love is always heard.

*Y*our imperfections are what make you beautiful.

Sandra Bullock
布洛克

You can fall from the sky.
You can fall from a tree.
But the best way to fall
Is in love with me.

Anonymous
佚名

YOU *are the sun in my day, the wind in my sky, the waves in my ocean and the beat in my heart.*

Anonymous
佚名

You're my shooting star because everything I've ever wished for is everything you are.

Anonymous
佚名

You *can love and love as many times as you want... but with the same person.*

Anonymous
佚名

You are worth every breathing moment of every day, of each week, of all *12* months, of each year to come. You are worth my life.

Anonymous
佚名

YOU don't stop loving someone, if you do, you never really loved them!

Anonymous
佚名

*Y*ou are the everlasting fire in the empty torch of my heart and the beacon of light which guides my vessel to your safe harbor.

Anonymous
佚名

You could put all the hearts together in the world and that still wouldn't describe how much I love you.

Anonymous
佚名

Wisdom

智慧

A friend is someone who knows the song in your heart and can sing it back to you when you have forgotten the words.

nonymous
佚名

A friend is someone who can see the truth and pain in you even when you are fooling everyone else.

Anonymous
佚名

Always be a first-rate version of yourself, instead of a second-rate version of somebody else.

Judy Garland, American actress and singer, 1922-1969
加兰,美国演员,歌手

A true friend is someone who sees the pain in your eyes while everyone else believes the smile on your face

Alex
阿莱克斯

Advice is what we ask for when we already know the answer but wish we didn't.

Erica Jong
埃里卡·雍

A great many people think they are thinking when they are merely rearranging their prejudices.

William James, American psychologist and philosopher, 1842-1910

威廉·詹姆斯,美国心理学家、哲学家

A long habit of not thinking a thing wrong, gives it a superficial appearance of being right.

Thomas Paine, American author and revolutionary leader, 1737-1809

潘恩,美国作家,革命领袖

A wise man's question contains half the answer.

Solomon Ibn Gabriel

加布里埃尔

A wise person knows that there is something to be learned from **everyone**.

Anonymous

侠名

A fool flatters himself, a wise man flatters the fool.

Edward G. Bulwer-Lytton, British author, 1803-1873

布尔-利顿,英国作家

A wise man gets more use from his enemies than a fool from his friends.

Baltasar Gracian, Spanish philosopher, writer, 1601-1658
格拉斯昂,西班牙哲学家、作家

A fool sees not the same tree that a wise man sees.

William Blake, British poet, artist, 1757-1827
布雷克,英国诗人、艺术家

A crowd has the collective wisdom of individual ignorance.

Thomas Carlyle, Scottish essayist, historian, 1795 -1881
卡莱尔,苏格兰散文家、历史学家

A cruel story runs on wheels, and every hand oils the wheels as they run.

Ouida, English novelist, social critic, 1839-1908
奎达,英国小说家、社会批评家

A good country song takes a page out of somebody's life and puts it to music.

Conway Twitty, American singer, 1946 -
特威蒂,美国歌手

A good writer does not write as people write, but as he writes.

Charles Montesquieu, South African golfer, 1935 –
孟德斯鸠,南非高尔夫球员

A hole is **nothing** at all, but you can break your neck in it.

Austin O'Malley, American physician, humorist, 1858-1932
奥马雷,美国医生、幽默家

A journey of a thousand miles starts in front of your feet.

Lao Zi, Chinese philosopher.
老子,中国哲学家

A lost battle is a battle one thinks one has lost.

Ferdinand Foch, French field marshal, 1851-1929
福赫,法国元帅

A loving heart is the truest wisdom.

Charles Dickens, English novelist, dramatist, 1812-1870
狄更斯,英国小说家、剧作家

A man is never the same for long. He is continually changing. He seldom remains the same even for half an hour.

George Gurdjieff, Russian teacher, writer, 1872-1949
古尔捷耶夫,俄罗斯教师、作家

A perfect human being: Man in search of his ideal of perfection. Nothing less.

Pir Vilayat Inayat Khan
卡恩

A poem begins in delight and ends in wisdom.

Robert Frost, American poet, 1874-1963
弗罗斯特,美国诗人

A proverb is one man's wit and all men's wisdom.

John Russell, American architect, 1895-1983
约翰·罗素,美国建筑师

A song is a poem set to music.

Tom T. Hall, American singer, songwriter, 1936-
霍尔,美国歌手、作曲家

A traveler without observation is a bird without wings.

Moslih Eddin Saadi Persian poet, 1184-1291

萨迪,波斯诗人

A strong, positive self-image is the best possible preparation for success.

Joyce Brothers, American psychologist, author, 1928 -

布拉泽斯,美国心理学家、作家

Accept that all of us can be hurt, that all of us can — and surely will at times — fail. I think we should follow a simple rule: if we can take the worst, take the risk.

Joyce Brothers, American psychologist, author, 1928-

布拉泽斯,美国心理学家、作家

Animals, in their generation, are wiser than the sons of men; but their wisdom is confined to a few particulars, and lies

in a *very narrow* compass.

Joseph Addison, English essayist, poet, statesman, 1672-1719

艾迪生,英国散文家、诗人、政治家

A good traveler has no fixed plans, and is not intent on arriving.

Lao Zi, Chinese philosopher.
老子，中国哲学家

Art is a marriage of the conscious and the unconscious.

Jean Cocteau, French author, 1981-1963
科克托，法国作家

***A closed mind is like a closed book*;** *just a block of wood.*

Chinese proverb
中国谚语

An age is called Dark, not because the light fails to shine, but because people refuse to see it.

James A. Michener
詹姆斯·米切纳

A journey of a thousand miles begins with a single step.

Chinese proverb
中国谚语

Beauty is *not* caused. It is.

Emily Dickinson, American poet, 1830-1836
艾米丽·迪金森,美国诗人

Believe those who are seeking the truth; doubt those who find it.

Andre Gide, French writer, 1869-1951
纪德,法国作家

Before your dreams can come true, you have to have those dreams.

Joyce Brothers, American psychologist, author, 1928-
布拉泽斯,美国心理学家、作家

Being sad with the right *people* is better than being happy with the wrong ones.

Philippos
菲利波斯

Beer the cause of and solution to all of life's little problems.

Homer Simpson
辛普森

Be wiser than other people, if you can, but do not tell them so.

Chesterfield British statesman and author, 1694-1773
切斯特菲尔德，英国政治家，作家

Better to understand a little than to misunderstand a lot.

Anonymous
佚名

Build a system that even a fool can use, and only a fool will want to use it.

George Bernard Shaw, British playwright and critic, 1856-1950
萧伯纳，英国剧作家、批评家

Be who you are and say what you feel because those who mind don't matter and those who matter don't mind.

Dr. Seuss
瑟斯医生

By three methods we may learn wisdom:
first, by reflection which is noblest;
second, by imitation, which is the easiest; and third, by experience, which is
the bitterest.

Confucius, Chinese philosopher and educator
孔子,中国哲学家、教育家

Change your thoughts and you change your world.

Norman Vincent Peale
诺曼·皮尔

Caring for others is great. Sometimes not-caring can
also be a kind of care.

Hans Taeger
汉斯·泰格

Cleverness is not wisdom.

Euripidese, Greek dramatist, 480-406 B.C.
欧里庇得斯,希腊剧作家

Common sense is not so common.

Jessica Truman
杰西卡·杜鲁门

Don't take life too serious. You'll never escape it alive anyway.

Elbert Hubbard, American writer, 1856-1915
埃尔伯特·哈伯德,美国作家

Don't waste your time on someone who isn't willing to waste their time on you...

Anonymous
佚名

Don't play stupid with me...I'm better at it.

Anonymous
佚名

Don't forget. I'm just a girl standing in front of a boy...*asking* him to love her.

Julia Roberts
朱莉亚·罗伯茨

𝒟on't cry because it is over; smile because it happened!

Gabriel Garcia Marquez
马奎兹

Doing easily what others find difficult is talent; doing what is impossible for talent is genius.

Henri-Frederic Amiel
阿米尔

Don't criticize what you can't understand.

Bob Dylan, American musician, 1941-
鲍勃·迪伦,美国音乐家

Education's purpose is to replace an empty mind with an open mind.

Malcolm S. Forbes
福布斯

Every fool knows you can't touch the stars, but it doesn't stop a wise man from trying.

Harry Anderson
哈里·安德森

Every man gets a narrower and narrower field of knowledge in which he must be an expert in order to compete with other people. The specialist knows more and more about less and less and finally knows everything about nothing.

Konrad Lorenz
康拉德·洛伦斯

Every great achievement was once considered impossible.

Everyone hears what you say. Friends listen to what you say. Best friends listen to what you don't say.

Everything has beauty, but not everyone sees it.

Confucius, Chinese philosopher.
孔子,中国哲学家

Even a fool may be wise after the event.

Homer, Greek poet
荷马,希腊诗人

Fools give you reasons, wise men never try.

Oscar Hammerstein II, American lyricist, 1895-1960
哈默斯坦,美国歌词作者

Few people think more than two or three times a year; I have made an international reputation for myself by thinking once or twice a week.

George Bernard Shaw, British playwright and critic, 1856-1950
萧伯纳，英国剧作家、批评家

Genius is one percent inspiration and ninety-nine percent perspiration.

Thomas Edison, American inventor, 1847-1931
爱迪生，美国发明家

Great is the man who does not lose his child mind.

Meng-Ts, Chinese thinker and educator
孟子，中国思想家、教育家

Good people are good because they've come to wisdom through failure. We get very little wisdom from success, you know.

William Saroyan, American author, 1884-1956
萨罗扬，美国作家

God grants me the serenity to accept the things I cannot change, courage to change the things I can, and wisdom to know the difference.

The Serenity Prayer
祈祷书

Great minds discuss ideas; Average minds discuss events; Small minds discuss *people*.

Eleanor Roosevelt
埃莉诺·罗斯福

Have you ever wondered which hurts the most: saying something and wishing you had not, or saying nothing, and wishing you had?

Anonymous
佚名

However many holy words you read, how many you speak, what good will they do you if you do not act upon them?

The Buddha
佛陀

It is by no means the least of life's rules: To let things alone.

Baltasar Gracian, Spanish philosopher, writer, 1601-1658
格拉斯昂,西班牙哲学家、作家

I'm a nobody, nobody is perfect, and therefore I am perfect!

Anonymous
佚名

In the frank expression of conflicting opinions lies the greatest promise of wisdom in governmental action.

Louis Dembitz Brandeis, Justice American Supreme Court, 1856-1941
布兰代斯，美国最高法院法官

I see no wisdom in saving up indignation for a rainy day.

Heywood Broun, American journalist,
1888-1939
布龙，美国记者

It's not whether you get knocked down. Its whether you get up **again.**

Vince Lombardi
隆巴迪

If you count all the stars in the sky, all the grains of sand in the oceans, all the roses in the world and all the smiles that have ever been, then you will have a

sample of how much *I love you.*

Philip
菲利普

In the end, it's not going to matter how many breaths you took, but how many moments took your breath away.

Anonymous
佚名

It is astonishing with how little wisdom mankind can be governed, when that little wisdom is its own.

William Ralph Inge, British writer, 1860-1954
威廉·拉尔夫·英,英国作家

It requires wisdom to understand wisdom: the music is nothing if the audience is deaf.

Walter Lippman
利普曼

It's better to **keep** your mouth shut and give the impression that you're stupid than to open it and remove all doubt.

Rami Belson
贝尔森

I have not failed. I've just found 10,000 ways that won't work.

Thomas Alva Edison, American inventor, 1847-1931
爱迪生,美国发明家

It's only after someone is gone do **you** realize how much you miss them...

Anonymous
佚名

I can only please one person per day. Today isn't your day...and tomorrow doesn't look good either.

Anonymous
佚名

I am not a vegetarian because I love animals; I am a vegetarian because I hate plants.

A. Whitney Brown
布朗

If you don't make mistakes, you aren't really trying.

Coleman Hawking
霍金

I'm trying really hard not to cry over you **because** every tear is just one more reminder that I don't know how to let you go.

Anonymous
佚名

I always knew looking back on the tears would make me laugh, but I never knew looking back on the laughs would make *me cry* .

Anonymous
佚名

It takes a minute to have a crush on someone, an hour to like someone, and a day to love someone — but it takes a lifetime to forget someone.

Anonymous
佚名

I am enough of an artist to draw freely upon my imagination.

Albert Einstein, American theoretical physicist, philosopher, 1875-1955
爱因斯坦,美国理论物理学家、哲学家

I *hate* quotations. Tell me what you know.

Ralph Waldo Emerson, American author, 1803-1882
爱默生,美国作家

I never make stupid mistakes. Only very, very clever ones.

John Peel
约翰·皮尔

It's not what you know; it's what you do with what you *know*.

Anonymous
佚名

I was gratified to be able to answer promptly. I said, "I don't know".

Mark Twain, American writer and humorist, 1835-1910
马克·吐温, 美国作家、幽默家

If the human mind was simple enough to understand, we'd be too simple to **understand it.**

Emerson Pugh
爱默生·皮尤

Ignorance of one's misfortunes is clear gain.

Euripidese, Greek dramatist, 480-406 B.C.
欧里庇得斯, 希腊剧作家

In just two days, **tomorrow** will be yesterday...

Anonymous
佚名

I'll soon get over us, this I know is true, then the day you start wanting me, I wont be wanting you, someday you'll remember, someday when your free, memories will remind you, that we were meant to be!

Baby Gangsta
巴比·甘斯达

Live as if your were to die tomorrow... Learn as if you were to live forever.

Mahatma Gandhi, Hindu nationalist and spiritual leader，1869-1948
甘地,印度民族解放运动领袖

Life is a constant challenge to know oneself.

Sri Rajneesh
拉杰尼士

Life moves pretty fast. If you don't stop and look around once in a while, you could miss it.

Ferris Bueller
费里斯·比勒

Learning makes the wise wiser and the fool more foolish.

John Ray, British pioneer naturalist, 1627-1705
约翰·雷，英国博物学家先驱

Let us be thankful for the fools. But for them the rest of us could not succeed.

Mark Twain, American writer and humorist, 1835-1910
马克·吐温，美国作家、幽默家

More than any time in history mankind faces a cross-roads. One path leads to despair and utter hopeless-ness, the other to total extinction. Let us pray that we have the wisdom to choose correctly.

Woody Allen, American movie actor, comedian, director, 1935-
伍迪·艾伦，美国电影演员、喜剧演员、导演

Nothing has really happened until it has been recorded.

Virginia Woolf, English author, 1882-1941
伍尔夫，英国作家

Never tell your problems to anyone…20% don't care and the other 80% are glad you have them.

Lou Holtz
霍尔茨

Never frown because you never know who might be falling in love with your smile.

Anonymous
佚名

No matter where you *go*, there you are.

Jackie Mason, American comedian
杰基·梅森,美国当代喜剧家

Never explain yourself. Your friends don't need it and your enemies won't believe it.

Belgicia Howell
豪厄尔

Never regret. If it's good, it's wonderful. If it's bad, it's *experience*.

Victoria Holt, writer
维多利亚·霍尔特,作家

Never **underestimate the power of stupid people in large groups.**

Anonymous
佚名

Our character is what we do when we think no one is looking.

Anonymous
佚名

One fool can ask more questions in a minute than twelve wise men can answer in an hour.

Nikolai Lenin
列宁

Only dead fish go with the current.

Anonymous
佚名

Once I dropped a tear in the ocean, the day I find it is the day I'll stop loving you

Anonymous
佚名

People will forget what you said.
People will forget what you did.
But people will never forget how you made them feel.

Anonymous
佚名

People have the right to be stupid. Some people abuse that privilege.

Anonymous
佚名

Peace cannot be achieved through violence; it can only be attained through understanding.

Albert Einstein, American theoretical physicist, philosopher, 1875-1955
爱因斯坦,美国理论物理学家、哲学家

People have one thing in common: they are all different.

Robert Zend
罗伯特·曾德

Question everything. Learn something. Answer nothing.

Engineer's Motto
工程师的格言

Reality can destroy the dream; why shouldn't the dream destroy reality?

George Moore
乔治·穆尔

Should I smile because we are friends? Or cry because we'll never be anything more?

Anonymous
佚名

Someday someone might come into your life and love you the way you've always wanted. If your someday was yesterday, learn. If your someday is tomorrow, hope. If your someday is today, cherish.

Anonymous
佚名

Some cause happiness wherever they go; others whenever they go.

Oscar Wilde, Irish writer, playwright, 1854-1900
王尔德,爱尔兰作家、剧作家

Sometimes my mind wanders; other times it leaves completely.

Anonymous
佚名

Silence is foolish if we are wise, but wise if we are foolish.

Charles Caleb Colton, English writer, cleric, merchant, 1780-1832
查尔斯·科尔顿,英国作家、修士、商人

Suicide is killing the ONE person you can actually change。

Sherris
舍里斯

Sometimes, when you're mad, you have the right to be mad, but you don't have the right to be cruel.

Anonymous
佚名

Silence is foolish if we are wise, but wise if we are foolish.

Charles Caleb Colton, English writer, cleric, merchant, 1780-1832
查尔斯·科尔顿,英国作家、修士、商人

Some of the waiters discuss the menu with you as if they were sharing wisdom picked up in the Himalayas.

Seymour Britchky
布里奇

There is but one way to be born but a hundred ways to die.

Chinese Proverb
中国谚语

The mind's direction is more important than its progress.

Joseph Joubert
约瑟夫·朱伯特

To do is to be.

Socrates, Greek philosopher, 470-399 B.C.
苏格拉底,希腊哲学家

To be is to do.

Plato, Greek philosopher, 4th century BC
柏拉图，希腊哲学家

The **way** to do is to be.

Lao Zi, Chinese philosopher
老子，中国哲学家

The greatest wealth is a poverty of desires.

Lucius Annaeus Seneca, Roman philosopher
塞尼卡，罗马哲学家

The greatest gift you can give another is the purity of your attention.

Richard Moss
里查德·莫斯

The most unchangeable truth is change.

Hans Taeger
汉斯·泰格

253

The foolish man seeks happiness in the distance, the wise grows it under his feet.

J. Robert Oppenheimer, American physicist, 1904-1967

奥彭海默,美国物理学家

The fool thinks **himself** to be wise, but the wise man knows himself to be a fool.

William Shakespeare, English playwright and poet, 1564-1616

莎士比亚,英国剧作家、诗人

There are times when fear is *good*. It must keep its watchful place at the heart's controls. There is advantage in the wisdom won from pain.

Chylus, Greek dramatist, 525-456 BC

奇拉斯,希腊剧作家

The attempt to combine wisdom and power has only rarely been successful and then only for a *short* while.

George Baker, American religious leader, 1877-1965

乔治·贝克,美国宗教领袖

To profit from good advice requires more wisdom than to give it.

Churton Collins
科林斯

These days people seek knowledge, not wisdom. Knowledge is of the past, wisdom is of the future.

Andre Gide, French writer, 1869-1951
纪德,法国作家

The mistakes of the fool are known to the world, but not to himself. The mistakes of the wise man are known to himself, but not to the world.

Charles Caleb Colton, English writer 1780-1832
查尔斯·科尔顿,英国作家

The *heart* of a fool is in his mouth, but the mouth of a wise man is in his heart.

Benjamin Franklin, American statesman, diplomat, 1706-1790
富兰克林,美国政治家、外交家

This **world** is a comedy for those who think and a tragedy for those who feel.

Horace, Roman poet, 65-68 B.C.
贺拉斯,罗马诗人

There comes a point in your life when you realize who really matters, who never did, and who always will.

Anonymous
佚名

The future belongs to those who believe in the beauty of their dreams.

Eleanor Roosevelt, American diplomat, author, 1884-1962
埃莉诺·罗斯福,美国外交家、作家

The mistakes of the fool are known to the world, but not to himself. The mistakes of the wise man are known to himself, but not to the world.

Charles Caleb Colton, English writer, 1780-1832
查尔斯·科尔顿,英国作家

The **heart** of a fool is in his mouth, but the mouth of a wise man is in his heart.

Benjamin Franklin, American statesman, diplomat,
1706-1790
富兰克林,美国政治家、外交家

To succeed in the world it is not enough to be stupid, you must also be well mannered.

Voltaire, French philosopher, 1604-1778
伏尔泰,法国哲学家

Truly great madness can not be achieved without significant intelligence.

Henrik Tikkanen

Truly great friends are hard to find, difficult to leave, and impossible to forget.

G. Randolf
伦道夫

Trying is the first step towards failure.

Homer Simpson
辛普森

The truth is more important than the facts.

Frank Lloyd Wright, 1868-1959
莱特

The trouble with the world is that the stupid are cocksure and the intelligent are full of doubt.

Bertrand Russell, British philosopher, 1872-1970
罗素,英国哲学家

The shortest word I know is "I". The sweetest word I know is "**LOVE**". And the person I never forget is "YOU".

Ervee Rios
莱欧斯

To meet girl in park is good, but to park meat in girl is better.

Confucius, Chinese philosopher and educator
孔子,中国哲学家、教育家

The true measure of a man is how he treats someone who can do him absolutely no *good*.

Ann Landers
安·兰德斯

The worst feeling you'll ever feel is sitting **next** to the person who means the world to you knowing that you mean nothing to them.

Anonymous
佚名

The real art of conversation is not only to say the right thing at the right time, but also to leave unsaid the wrong thing at the tempting moment.

Anonymous
佚名

There is no such thing as a stupid question, just stupid *people* who ask questions.

Anonymous
佚名

The art of being wise is the art of knowing what to

overlook.

William James, American psychologist and philosopher, 1842-1910
威廉·詹姆斯，美国心理学家、哲学家

The important thing is not to stop questioning. Curiosity has its own reason for existing.

Albert Einstein, American theoretical physicist, philosopher, 1875-1955
爱因斯坦,美国理论物理学家、哲学家

The *most* incomprehensible thing about the world is that it is at all comprehensible.

Albert Einstein, American theoretical physicist, philosopher, 1875-1955
爱因斯坦,美国理论物理学家、哲学家

The only true wisdom is in knowing you know *nothing*.

Socrates, Greek philosopher, 470-399 B.C.
苏格拉底,希腊哲学家

There are three types of people in this world: those who make things happen, those who watch things happen and those who wonder what **happened.**

Mary Kay Ash
阿什

The worst way to miss someone is to be sitting right beside them knowing you can't have them.

Anonymous

佚名

What do you do when the only one that can make you stop crying, is the person who made you cry?

Anonymous

佚名

When you are educated, you'll believe only half of what you hear. When you're intelligent, you know which half.

Jerome Perryman

杰罗姆·佩里曼

What you are is what you have been, and what you will be is what you do now.

The Buddha

佛陀

When I get a little money I buy books; and if any is left I buy food and clothes.

Erasmus, Swiss theoloian and philosopher, 1524-1583

伊拉斯膜,瑞士神学家、哲学家

Wise men learn by other men's mistakes, fools by their own.

H. G. Bohn
波恩

When you check your own mind properly, you stop blaming others for your problems.

Lama Thubten Yeshe
耶什

Wisdom begins in *wonder*.

Socrates, Greek philosopher, 470-399 B. C.
苏格拉底,希腊哲学家

We come to love not by finding a perfect person, but by learning to see an imperfect person perfectly.

Sam Keen
基恩

Wise men talk because they have something to say; fools, because they have to say something.

Plato, Greek philosopher, 4th cenruty B. C.
柏拉图,希腊哲学家

We are all either fools or undiscovered geniuses.

Bonnie Lin
邦尼·林

Work like you don't need the money, love like you've never been hurt and dance like no one is watching.

Randall G Leighton
莱顿

Wisdom stands at the turn in the road and calls upon us publicly, but we consider it false and despise its adherents.

Kahlil Gibran, Lebanon poet, philosopher and artist, 1883-1931
纪伯伦,黎巴嫩诗人、哲学家、艺术家

Wise men don't need advice. Fools won't take it.

Benjamin Franklin, American statesman, diplomat
1706-1790
富兰克林,美国政治家、外交家

When a person can no longer laugh at himself, it is time for others to laugh at him.

Thomas S. Szasz, American psychiatrist
托马斯·萨兹,美国当代精神病学家

YOU tried your best and failed miserably. The lesson is, "never try".

You can tell whether a man is clever by his answers. You can tell whether a man is wise by his questions.

You don't love a woman because she is beautiful; she is beautiful because you love her.

You miss 100% **of the shots you don't take.**

You were not born a winner, and you were not born a loser. You are what you make **yourself** be.

Yesterday is history. Tomorrow is a mystery. Today is a gift. That's why it's called the present.

Anonymous
佚名

You *must* experience and accept the extremes. Because if the contrast is lost, you lose appreciation; and when you lose appreciation, you lose the value of everything.

Philippos
菲利波斯

图书在版编目（CIP）数据

英汉对照·心灵阅读. 7, 箴言篇/林立，陈爱明，李小艳编译. ——北京：外文出版社，2004

ISBN 7 – 119 – 03741 – 2

Ⅰ. 英… Ⅱ. ①林… ②陈… ③李… Ⅲ. 英语—对照读物，英、汉 Ⅳ. H319.4

中国版本图书馆 CIP 数据核字（2004）第 058188 号

外文出版社网址：
　http://www.flp.com.cn
外文出版社电子信箱：
　info@flp.com.cn
　sales@flp.com.cn

英汉对照·心灵阅读（七）

箴　言　篇

编　　译　林　立　陈爱明　李小艳
审　　校　韩清月

责任编辑　王　蕊
封面设计　张　蕾
印刷监制　张国祥
出版发行　外文出版社
社　　址　北京市百万庄大街24号　　　邮政编码　100037
电　　话　（010）68995963（编辑部）
　　　　　（010）68329514/68327211（推广发行部）
印　　刷　北京中印联印务有限公司
经　　销　新华书店/外文书店
开　　本　大32开　　　　　　　　字　　数　100千字
印　　数　10001—15000册　　　　　印　　张　8.5
版　　次　2006年3月第1版第2次印刷
装　　别　平
书　　号　ISBN 7 – 119 – 03741 – 2 /H·1627（外）
定　　价　15.80元